50 Finland Pizza Recipes for Home

By: Kelly Johnson

Table of Contents

- Classic Margherita Pizza
- Mushroom and Cheese Pizza
- Pepperoni Pizza
- Hawaiian Pizza
- Four Cheese Pizza
- Spinach and Feta Pizza
- BBQ Chicken Pizza
- Veggie Supreme Pizza
- Meat Lovers Pizza
- Prosciutto and Arugula Pizza
- Mediterranean Pizza
- Bacon and Egg Breakfast Pizza
- Taco Pizza
- Pesto Chicken Pizza
- Capricciosa Pizza
- Buffalo Chicken Pizza
- White Pizza with Ricotta and Spinach
- Sausage and Peppers Pizza
- Chicken Alfredo Pizza
- Shrimp Scampi Pizza
- Greek Pizza
- Artichoke and Olive Pizza
- Roasted Vegetable Pizza
- Smoked Salmon Pizza
- Fig and Goat Cheese Pizza
- Blue Cheese and Pear Pizza
- Margherita with Balsamic Glaze Pizza
- Potato and Rosemary Pizza
- Pumpkin and Sage Pizza
- Beef and Blue Cheese Pizza
- Reindeer Sausage Pizza
- Clam and Garlic Pizza
- Chicken Tikka Masala Pizza
- Apple and Cheddar Pizza
- Mushroom and Truffle Oil Pizza

- Pear and Gorgonzola Pizza
- Swedish Meatball Pizza
- Chicken Caesar Pizza
- Kimchi Pizza
- Breakfast Pizza with Sausage and Egg
- Smoked Trout Pizza
- Grilled Vegetable and Hummus Pizza
- Pastrami and Swiss Pizza
- Steak and Blue Cheese Pizza
- Ratatouille Pizza
- Curry Chicken Pizza
- Avocado and Bacon Pizza
- Brussels Sprouts and Pancetta Pizza
- Beet and Goat Cheese Pizza
- Lingonberry and Brie Pizza

Classic Margherita Pizza

Ingredients:

For the pizza dough:

- 2 1/4 teaspoons (1 packet) active dry yeast
- 1 1/2 cups warm water (about 110°F/45°C)
- 4 cups all-purpose flour
- 1 teaspoon sugar
- 1 1/2 teaspoons salt
- 2 tablespoons olive oil, plus more for greasing

For the toppings:

- 1/2 cup pizza sauce or marinara sauce
- 8 ounces fresh mozzarella cheese, sliced
- 2-3 medium-sized tomatoes, thinly sliced
- Fresh basil leaves
- Salt and pepper to taste
- Extra-virgin olive oil, for drizzling

Instructions:

Prepare the Pizza Dough:
- In a small bowl, dissolve the yeast in warm water and let it sit for about 5 minutes until frothy.
- In a large mixing bowl, combine the flour, sugar, and salt. Make a well in the center and add the yeast mixture and olive oil.
- Stir the mixture until a dough forms. Turn the dough out onto a floured surface and knead for about 5-7 minutes until smooth and elastic.
- Place the dough in a lightly greased bowl, cover with a clean kitchen towel or plastic wrap, and let it rise in a warm place for about 1-1.5 hours until doubled in size.

Preheat the Oven:
- Preheat your oven to 475°F (245°C). If you have a pizza stone, place it in the oven while it preheats.

Shape the Dough:

- Punch down the risen dough and divide it into two equal portions for two pizzas. On a lightly floured surface, roll out each portion of dough into a circle about 10-12 inches in diameter.

Assemble the Pizza:
- Place the rolled-out dough onto a pizza peel or a lightly greased baking sheet.
- Spread half of the pizza sauce evenly over the dough, leaving a small border around the edges.
- Arrange the sliced tomatoes over the sauce, followed by the slices of fresh mozzarella.
- Tear fresh basil leaves and scatter them over the top of the pizza.
- Season with salt and pepper to taste.

Bake the Pizza:
- If using a pizza stone, carefully transfer the assembled pizza onto the preheated stone in the oven. If using a baking sheet, place the baking sheet with the pizza directly in the oven.
- Bake for 10-12 minutes, or until the crust is golden brown and the cheese is bubbly and slightly browned.

Serve:
- Remove the pizza from the oven and let it cool slightly.
- Drizzle with extra-virgin olive oil before serving.
- Slice and enjoy your classic Margherita Pizza!

Feel free to adjust the toppings or add extra ingredients according to your preference. Buon appetito!

Mushroom and Cheese Pizza

Ingredients:

For the Pizza Dough:

- 1 pound (about 4 cups) pizza dough, store-bought or homemade
- Cornmeal or flour for dusting

For the Pizza Toppings:

- 1 cup pizza sauce or marinara sauce
- 2 cups shredded mozzarella cheese
- 1 cup sliced mushrooms (such as cremini or button mushrooms)
- 1/2 cup sliced red onion
- 2 cloves garlic, minced
- 1 tablespoon olive oil
- Salt and pepper to taste
- Crushed red pepper flakes (optional)
- Fresh basil leaves, torn, for garnish (optional)
- Grated Parmesan cheese, for serving (optional)

Instructions:

Preheat the Oven:
- Preheat your oven to the highest temperature it can go, typically around 475-500°F (245-260°C). If you have a pizza stone, place it in the oven to preheat as well.

Prepare the Toppings:
- In a skillet, heat olive oil over medium heat. Add sliced mushrooms, sliced red onion, minced garlic, salt, and pepper. Cook, stirring occasionally, until the mushrooms are golden brown and the onions are softened, about 5-7 minutes. Remove from heat and set aside.

Stretch the Dough:
- Dust a work surface with cornmeal or flour. Place the pizza dough on the surface and gently stretch it into a round or rectangular shape, about 12-14 inches in diameter.

Assemble the Pizza:
- Transfer the stretched pizza dough to a pizza peel or parchment paper-lined baking sheet.

- Spread pizza sauce evenly over the dough, leaving a small border around the edges.
- Sprinkle shredded mozzarella cheese over the sauce.
- Distribute the cooked mushroom and onion mixture evenly over the cheese.

Bake the Pizza:
- If using a pizza stone, carefully transfer the pizza from the peel to the preheated stone in the oven. If using a baking sheet, simply place the baking sheet in the oven.
- Bake the pizza for 10-12 minutes, or until the crust is golden brown and the cheese is melted and bubbly.

Finish and Serve:
- Remove the pizza from the oven and let it cool slightly.
- If desired, sprinkle crushed red pepper flakes over the pizza for added heat.
- Garnish with torn fresh basil leaves and grated Parmesan cheese, if desired.
- Slice the pizza and serve hot.

Notes:

- Feel free to customize your pizza with additional toppings like sliced bell peppers, olives, or fresh herbs.
- You can use any type of cheese you prefer or a combination of cheeses for extra flavor.
- Adjust the cooking time depending on your oven and desired level of crispiness for the crust.

Enjoy your delicious homemade mushroom and cheese pizza!

Pepperoni Pizza

Ingredients:

For the Pizza Dough:

- 1 pound (about 4 cups) pizza dough, store-bought or homemade
- Cornmeal or flour for dusting

For the Pizza Toppings:

- 1 cup pizza sauce or marinara sauce
- 2 cups shredded mozzarella cheese
- 1/2 cup sliced pepperoni
- Crushed red pepper flakes (optional)
- Fresh basil leaves, torn, for garnish (optional)
- Grated Parmesan cheese, for serving (optional)

Instructions:

Preheat the Oven:
- Preheat your oven to the highest temperature it can go, typically around 475-500°F (245-260°C). If you have a pizza stone, place it in the oven to preheat as well.

Stretch the Dough:
- Dust a work surface with cornmeal or flour. Place the pizza dough on the surface and gently stretch it into a round or rectangular shape, about 12-14 inches in diameter.

Assemble the Pizza:
- Transfer the stretched pizza dough to a pizza peel or parchment paper-lined baking sheet.
- Spread pizza sauce evenly over the dough, leaving a small border around the edges.
- Sprinkle shredded mozzarella cheese evenly over the sauce.
- Arrange sliced pepperoni over the cheese.

Bake the Pizza:
- If using a pizza stone, carefully transfer the pizza from the peel to the preheated stone in the oven. If using a baking sheet, simply place the baking sheet in the oven.

- Bake the pizza for 10-12 minutes, or until the crust is golden brown and the cheese is melted and bubbly.

Finish and Serve:
- Remove the pizza from the oven and let it cool slightly.
- If desired, sprinkle crushed red pepper flakes over the pizza for added heat.
- Garnish with torn fresh basil leaves and grated Parmesan cheese, if desired.
- Slice the pizza and serve hot.

Notes:

- Feel free to customize your pizza with additional toppings like sliced bell peppers, onions, or olives.
- You can use any type of cheese you prefer or a combination of cheeses for extra flavor.
- Adjust the cooking time depending on your oven and desired level of crispiness for the crust.

Enjoy your delicious homemade pepperoni pizza!

Hawaiian Pizza

Ingredients:

For the Pizza Dough:

- 1 pound (about 4 cups) pizza dough, store-bought or homemade
- Cornmeal or flour for dusting

For the Pizza Toppings:

- 1 cup pizza sauce or marinara sauce
- 2 cups shredded mozzarella cheese
- 1 cup diced cooked ham or Canadian bacon
- 1 cup diced pineapple (fresh or canned)
- Crushed red pepper flakes (optional)
- Fresh basil leaves, torn, for garnish (optional)
- Grated Parmesan cheese, for serving (optional)

Instructions:

Preheat the Oven:
- Preheat your oven to the highest temperature it can go, typically around 475-500°F (245-260°C). If you have a pizza stone, place it in the oven to preheat as well.

Stretch the Dough:
- Dust a work surface with cornmeal or flour. Place the pizza dough on the surface and gently stretch it into a round or rectangular shape, about 12-14 inches in diameter.

Assemble the Pizza:
- Transfer the stretched pizza dough to a pizza peel or parchment paper-lined baking sheet.
- Spread pizza sauce evenly over the dough, leaving a small border around the edges.
- Sprinkle shredded mozzarella cheese evenly over the sauce.
- Distribute diced ham or Canadian bacon and diced pineapple evenly over the cheese.

Bake the Pizza:
- If using a pizza stone, carefully transfer the pizza from the peel to the preheated stone in the oven. If using a baking sheet, simply place the baking sheet in the oven.

- Bake the pizza for 10-12 minutes, or until the crust is golden brown and the cheese is melted and bubbly.

Finish and Serve:
- Remove the pizza from the oven and let it cool slightly.
- If desired, sprinkle crushed red pepper flakes over the pizza for added heat.
- Garnish with torn fresh basil leaves and grated Parmesan cheese, if desired.
- Slice the pizza and serve hot.

Notes:

- You can use store-bought or homemade pizza dough for this recipe.
- If using canned pineapple, make sure to drain it well to remove excess juice.
- Feel free to add additional toppings such as sliced onions, bell peppers, or mushrooms if desired.

Enjoy your homemade Hawaiian pizza!

Four Cheese Pizza

Ingredients:

For the Pizza Dough:

- 1 pound (about 4 cups) pizza dough, store-bought or homemade
- Cornmeal or flour for dusting

For the Pizza Toppings:

- 1 cup pizza sauce or marinara sauce
- 1 cup shredded mozzarella cheese
- 1/2 cup shredded cheddar cheese
- 1/2 cup shredded provolone cheese
- 1/2 cup crumbled feta cheese
- Optional: additional toppings such as sliced tomatoes, caramelized onions, or fresh basil leaves

Instructions:

Preheat the Oven:
- Preheat your oven to the highest temperature it can go, typically around 475-500°F (245-260°C). If you have a pizza stone, place it in the oven to preheat as well.

Stretch the Dough:
- Dust a work surface with cornmeal or flour. Place the pizza dough on the surface and gently stretch it into a round or rectangular shape, about 12-14 inches in diameter.

Assemble the Pizza:
- Transfer the stretched pizza dough to a pizza peel or parchment paper-lined baking sheet.
- Spread pizza sauce evenly over the dough, leaving a small border around the edges.
- Sprinkle shredded mozzarella cheese evenly over the sauce.
- Scatter shredded cheddar cheese, shredded provolone cheese, and crumbled feta cheese over the mozzarella cheese.

Add Additional Toppings (Optional):
- If desired, add additional toppings such as sliced tomatoes, caramelized onions, or fresh basil leaves.

Bake the Pizza:
- If using a pizza stone, carefully transfer the pizza from the peel to the preheated stone in the oven. If using a baking sheet, simply place the baking sheet in the oven.
- Bake the pizza for 10-12 minutes, or until the crust is golden brown and the cheese is melted and bubbly.

Serve:
- Remove the pizza from the oven and let it cool slightly.
- Slice the pizza and serve hot.

Notes:

- You can use store-bought or homemade pizza dough for this recipe.
- Feel free to experiment with different types of cheeses based on your preferences. Other great options include gorgonzola, fontina, asiago, or goat cheese.
- Customize the pizza with your favorite toppings to create your own unique flavor combination.

Enjoy your delicious homemade four cheese pizza!

Spinach and Feta Pizza

Ingredients:

For the Pizza Dough:

- 1 pound (about 4 cups) pizza dough, store-bought or homemade
- Cornmeal or flour for dusting

For the Pizza Toppings:

- 1 cup pizza sauce or marinara sauce
- 2 cups shredded mozzarella cheese
- 1 cup crumbled feta cheese
- 2 cups fresh baby spinach leaves
- 2 cloves garlic, minced
- 1 tablespoon olive oil
- Salt and pepper to taste
- Crushed red pepper flakes (optional)
- Grated Parmesan cheese, for serving (optional)

Instructions:

Preheat the Oven:
- Preheat your oven to the highest temperature it can go, typically around 475-500°F (245-260°C). If you have a pizza stone, place it in the oven to preheat as well.

Prepare the Spinach:
- In a skillet, heat olive oil over medium heat. Add minced garlic and cook for 1 minute until fragrant.
- Add fresh baby spinach leaves to the skillet and cook, stirring occasionally, until wilted, about 2-3 minutes. Season with salt and pepper to taste. Remove from heat and set aside.

Stretch the Dough:
- Dust a work surface with cornmeal or flour. Place the pizza dough on the surface and gently stretch it into a round or rectangular shape, about 12-14 inches in diameter.

Assemble the Pizza:
- Transfer the stretched pizza dough to a pizza peel or parchment paper-lined baking sheet.

- Spread pizza sauce evenly over the dough, leaving a small border around the edges.
- Sprinkle shredded mozzarella cheese evenly over the sauce.
- Distribute wilted spinach evenly over the cheese.
- Crumble feta cheese over the top of the pizza.

Bake the Pizza:
- If using a pizza stone, carefully transfer the pizza from the peel to the preheated stone in the oven. If using a baking sheet, simply place the baking sheet in the oven.
- Bake the pizza for 10-12 minutes, or until the crust is golden brown and the cheese is melted and bubbly.

Finish and Serve:
- Remove the pizza from the oven and let it cool slightly.
- If desired, sprinkle crushed red pepper flakes over the pizza for added heat.
- Serve hot, optionally garnished with grated Parmesan cheese.

Notes:

- Feel free to add additional toppings such as sliced black olives, sliced tomatoes, or caramelized onions if desired.
- You can use store-bought or homemade pizza dough for this recipe.
- Adjust the cooking time depending on your oven and desired level of crispiness for the crust.

Enjoy your delicious homemade spinach and feta pizza!

BBQ Chicken Pizza

Ingredients:

For the Pizza Dough:

- 1 pound (about 4 cups) pizza dough, store-bought or homemade
- Cornmeal or flour for dusting

For the Pizza Toppings:

- 1 cup barbecue sauce (store-bought or homemade)
- 2 cups shredded cooked chicken (rotisserie chicken works well)
- 1 1/2 cups shredded mozzarella cheese
- 1/2 cup red onion, thinly sliced
- 1/4 cup fresh cilantro, chopped
- Optional: sliced jalapeños, cooked bacon pieces, or sliced bell peppers
- Optional: ranch or blue cheese dressing for drizzling

Instructions:

Preheat the Oven:
- Preheat your oven to the highest temperature it can go, typically around 475-500°F (245-260°C). If you have a pizza stone, place it in the oven to preheat as well.

Prepare the Pizza Dough:
- Dust a work surface with cornmeal or flour. Place the pizza dough on the surface and gently stretch it into a round or rectangular shape, about 12-14 inches in diameter.

Assemble the Pizza:
- Transfer the stretched pizza dough to a pizza peel or parchment paper-lined baking sheet.
- Spread barbecue sauce evenly over the dough, leaving a small border around the edges.
- Sprinkle shredded mozzarella cheese evenly over the sauce.
- Distribute shredded cooked chicken and thinly sliced red onion evenly over the cheese.
- Add any optional toppings such as sliced jalapeños, cooked bacon pieces, or sliced bell peppers.

Bake the Pizza:

- If using a pizza stone, carefully transfer the pizza from the peel to the preheated stone in the oven. If using a baking sheet, simply place the baking sheet in the oven.
- Bake the pizza for 10-12 minutes, or until the crust is golden brown and the cheese is melted and bubbly.

Finish and Serve:
- Remove the pizza from the oven and let it cool slightly.
- Sprinkle chopped fresh cilantro over the top of the pizza.
- Drizzle ranch or blue cheese dressing over the pizza, if desired.
- Slice the pizza and serve hot.

Notes:

- Adjust the amount of barbecue sauce according to your taste preferences. You can use more or less depending on how saucy you like your pizza.
- Feel free to customize your pizza with additional toppings such as pineapple, mushrooms, or different types of cheese.
- You can use store-bought or homemade pizza dough for this recipe.

Enjoy your delicious homemade BBQ chicken pizza!

Veggie Supreme Pizza

Ingredients:

For the Pizza Dough:

- 1 pound (about 4 cups) pizza dough, store-bought or homemade
- Cornmeal or flour for dusting

For the Pizza Toppings:

- 1 cup pizza sauce or marinara sauce
- 2 cups shredded mozzarella cheese
- 1/2 cup sliced mushrooms
- 1/2 cup sliced bell peppers (any color)
- 1/2 cup sliced red onion
- 1/2 cup sliced black olives
- 1/2 cup sliced cherry tomatoes
- 1/4 cup sliced banana peppers or pepperoncini
- 1/4 cup artichoke hearts, chopped
- 2 cloves garlic, minced
- 1 tablespoon olive oil
- Salt and pepper to taste
- Crushed red pepper flakes (optional)
- Grated Parmesan cheese, for serving (optional)
- Fresh basil leaves, torn, for garnish (optional)

Instructions:

Preheat the Oven:
- Preheat your oven to the highest temperature it can go, typically around 475-500°F (245-260°C). If you have a pizza stone, place it in the oven to preheat as well.

Prepare the Pizza Dough:
- Dust a work surface with cornmeal or flour. Place the pizza dough on the surface and gently stretch it into a round or rectangular shape, about 12-14 inches in diameter.

Assemble the Pizza:
- Transfer the stretched pizza dough to a pizza peel or parchment paper-lined baking sheet.

- Spread pizza sauce evenly over the dough, leaving a small border around the edges.
- Sprinkle shredded mozzarella cheese evenly over the sauce.
- Distribute sliced mushrooms, bell peppers, red onion, black olives, cherry tomatoes, banana peppers or pepperoncini, and chopped artichoke hearts evenly over the cheese.
- Sprinkle minced garlic over the top of the pizza.
- Drizzle olive oil over the vegetables. Season with salt and pepper to taste.

Bake the Pizza:
- If using a pizza stone, carefully transfer the pizza from the peel to the preheated stone in the oven. If using a baking sheet, simply place the baking sheet in the oven.
- Bake the pizza for 10-12 minutes, or until the crust is golden brown and the cheese is melted and bubbly.

Finish and Serve:
- Remove the pizza from the oven and let it cool slightly.
- If desired, sprinkle crushed red pepper flakes over the pizza for added heat.
- Garnish with grated Parmesan cheese and torn fresh basil leaves, if desired.
- Slice the pizza and serve hot.

Notes:

- Feel free to customize your pizza with additional toppings such as spinach, roasted red peppers, or different types of cheese.
- You can use store-bought or homemade pizza dough for this recipe.

Enjoy your delicious homemade veggie supreme pizza!

Meat Lovers Pizza

Ingredients:

For the Pizza Dough:

- 1 pound (about 4 cups) pizza dough, store-bought or homemade
- Cornmeal or flour for dusting

For the Pizza Toppings:

- 1 cup pizza sauce or marinara sauce
- 2 cups shredded mozzarella cheese
- 1/2 cup sliced pepperoni
- 1/2 cup cooked and crumbled Italian sausage
- 1/2 cup cooked and crumbled bacon
- 1/2 cup sliced ham or Canadian bacon
- 1/4 cup sliced black olives
- Optional: sliced jalapeños or banana peppers for added heat
- Optional: grated Parmesan cheese for serving

Instructions:

Preheat the Oven:
- Preheat your oven to the highest temperature it can go, typically around 475-500°F (245-260°C). If you have a pizza stone, place it in the oven to preheat as well.

Prepare the Pizza Dough:
- Dust a work surface with cornmeal or flour. Place the pizza dough on the surface and gently stretch it into a round or rectangular shape, about 12-14 inches in diameter.

Assemble the Pizza:
- Transfer the stretched pizza dough to a pizza peel or parchment paper-lined baking sheet.
- Spread pizza sauce evenly over the dough, leaving a small border around the edges.
- Sprinkle shredded mozzarella cheese evenly over the sauce.
- Distribute sliced pepperoni, cooked and crumbled Italian sausage, cooked and crumbled bacon, sliced ham or Canadian bacon, and sliced black olives evenly over the cheese.

- Add any optional toppings such as sliced jalapeños or banana peppers for added heat.

Bake the Pizza:
- If using a pizza stone, carefully transfer the pizza from the peel to the preheated stone in the oven. If using a baking sheet, simply place the baking sheet in the oven.
- Bake the pizza for 10-12 minutes, or until the crust is golden brown and the cheese is melted and bubbly.

Finish and Serve:
- Remove the pizza from the oven and let it cool slightly.
- Slice the pizza and serve hot.
- Sprinkle grated Parmesan cheese over the pizza, if desired.

Notes:

- Feel free to customize your meat lovers pizza with additional toppings such as cooked ground beef, sliced chicken, or different types of cheese.
- You can use store-bought or homemade pizza dough for this recipe.

Enjoy your delicious homemade meat lovers pizza!

Prosciutto and Arugula Pizza

Ingredients:

For the Pizza Dough:

- 1 pound (about 4 cups) pizza dough, store-bought or homemade
- Cornmeal or flour for dusting

For the Pizza Toppings:

- 1 cup pizza sauce or marinara sauce
- 2 cups shredded mozzarella cheese
- 4-6 slices prosciutto
- 2 cups fresh arugula
- 1 tablespoon extra virgin olive oil
- 1 teaspoon balsamic vinegar (optional)
- Salt and pepper to taste
- Grated Parmesan cheese for serving (optional)
- Red pepper flakes for serving (optional)

Instructions:

Preheat the Oven:
- Preheat your oven to the highest temperature it can go, typically around 475-500°F (245-260°C). If you have a pizza stone, place it in the oven to preheat as well.

Prepare the Pizza Dough:
- Dust a work surface with cornmeal or flour. Place the pizza dough on the surface and gently stretch it into a round or rectangular shape, about 12-14 inches in diameter.

Assemble the Pizza:
- Transfer the stretched pizza dough to a pizza peel or parchment paper-lined baking sheet.
- Spread pizza sauce evenly over the dough, leaving a small border around the edges.
- Sprinkle shredded mozzarella cheese evenly over the sauce.
- Tear or slice the prosciutto into smaller pieces and arrange them evenly over the cheese.

Bake the Pizza:

- If using a pizza stone, carefully transfer the pizza from the peel to the preheated stone in the oven. If using a baking sheet, simply place the baking sheet in the oven.
- Bake the pizza for 10-12 minutes, or until the crust is golden brown and the cheese is melted and bubbly.

Prepare the Arugula Topping:
- While the pizza is baking, toss the fresh arugula with extra virgin olive oil, balsamic vinegar (if using), salt, and pepper in a mixing bowl until evenly coated.

Finish and Serve:
- Remove the pizza from the oven and let it cool slightly.
- Spread the dressed arugula evenly over the baked pizza.
- Optionally, sprinkle grated Parmesan cheese and red pepper flakes over the top for added flavor and heat.
- Slice the pizza and serve hot.

Notes:

- Feel free to customize your prosciutto and arugula pizza with additional toppings such as sliced cherry tomatoes, caramelized onions, or shaved Parmesan cheese.
- You can use store-bought or homemade pizza dough for this recipe.

Enjoy your delicious homemade prosciutto and arugula pizza!

Mediterranean Pizza

Ingredients:

For the Pizza Dough:

- 1 pound (about 4 cups) pizza dough, store-bought or homemade
- Cornmeal or flour for dusting

For the Pizza Toppings:

- 1/2 cup pizza sauce or marinara sauce
- 1 cup shredded mozzarella cheese
- 1/2 cup crumbled feta cheese
- 1/4 cup sliced black olives
- 1/4 cup sliced Kalamata olives
- 1/2 cup sliced cherry tomatoes
- 1/4 cup chopped sun-dried tomatoes
- 1/4 cup sliced red onion
- 2 tablespoons chopped fresh basil or oregano
- 1 tablespoon extra virgin olive oil
- Salt and pepper to taste
- Crushed red pepper flakes (optional)

Instructions:

Preheat the Oven:
- Preheat your oven to the highest temperature it can go, typically around 475-500°F (245-260°C). If you have a pizza stone, place it in the oven to preheat as well.

Prepare the Pizza Dough:
- Dust a work surface with cornmeal or flour. Place the pizza dough on the surface and gently stretch it into a round or rectangular shape, about 12-14 inches in diameter.

Assemble the Pizza:
- Transfer the stretched pizza dough to a pizza peel or parchment paper-lined baking sheet.
- Spread pizza sauce evenly over the dough, leaving a small border around the edges.
- Sprinkle shredded mozzarella cheese evenly over the sauce.

- Scatter crumbled feta cheese, sliced black olives, sliced Kalamata olives, sliced cherry tomatoes, chopped sun-dried tomatoes, and sliced red onion over the cheese.
- Drizzle extra virgin olive oil over the toppings. Season with salt and pepper to taste.

Bake the Pizza:
- If using a pizza stone, carefully transfer the pizza from the peel to the preheated stone in the oven. If using a baking sheet, simply place the baking sheet in the oven.
- Bake the pizza for 10-12 minutes, or until the crust is golden brown and the cheese is melted and bubbly.

Finish and Serve:
- Remove the pizza from the oven and let it cool slightly.
- Sprinkle chopped fresh basil or oregano over the top of the pizza.
- Optionally, sprinkle crushed red pepper flakes over the pizza for added heat.
- Slice the pizza and serve hot.

Notes:

- Feel free to customize your Mediterranean pizza with additional toppings such as artichoke hearts, roasted red peppers, or capers.
- You can use store-bought or homemade pizza dough for this recipe.

Enjoy your delicious homemade Mediterranean pizza!

Bacon and Egg Breakfast Pizza

Ingredients:

For the Pizza Dough:

- 1 pound (about 4 cups) pizza dough, store-bought or homemade
- Cornmeal or flour for dusting

For the Pizza Toppings:

- 1 cup shredded mozzarella cheese
- 4 slices bacon, cooked until crispy and crumbled
- 4 large eggs
- Salt and pepper to taste
- 2 tablespoons chopped chives or green onions (optional)
- Grated Parmesan cheese for serving (optional)
- Red pepper flakes for serving (optional)

Instructions:

Preheat the Oven:
- Preheat your oven to the highest temperature it can go, typically around 475-500°F (245-260°C). If you have a pizza stone, place it in the oven to preheat as well.

Prepare the Pizza Dough:
- Dust a work surface with cornmeal or flour. Place the pizza dough on the surface and gently stretch it into a round or rectangular shape, about 12-14 inches in diameter.

Assemble the Pizza:
- Transfer the stretched pizza dough to a pizza peel or parchment paper-lined baking sheet.
- Sprinkle shredded mozzarella cheese evenly over the dough, leaving a small border around the edges.
- Scatter the cooked and crumbled bacon evenly over the cheese.
- Carefully crack the eggs onto the pizza, spacing them evenly apart. Be sure to leave some space around each egg to prevent them from running together.
- Season the eggs with salt and pepper to taste.

Bake the Pizza:

- If using a pizza stone, carefully transfer the pizza from the peel to the preheated stone in the oven. If using a baking sheet, simply place the baking sheet in the oven.
- Bake the pizza for 10-12 minutes, or until the crust is golden brown and the egg whites are set but the yolks are still slightly runny.

Finish and Serve:
- Remove the pizza from the oven and let it cool slightly.
- Sprinkle chopped chives or green onions over the top of the pizza.
- Optionally, sprinkle grated Parmesan cheese and red pepper flakes over the pizza for added flavor and heat.
- Slice the pizza and serve hot.

Notes:

- Be careful when cracking the eggs onto the pizza to avoid breaking the yolks.
- Feel free to customize your bacon and egg breakfast pizza with additional toppings such as sliced tomatoes, caramelized onions, or cooked spinach.
- You can use store-bought or homemade pizza dough for this recipe.

Enjoy your delicious homemade bacon and egg breakfast pizza!

Taco Pizza

Ingredients:

For the Pizza Dough:

- 1 pound (about 4 cups) pizza dough, store-bought or homemade
- Cornmeal or flour for dusting

For the Taco Toppings:

- 1 tablespoon olive oil
- 1 pound ground beef or turkey
- 1 packet (about 1 ounce) taco seasoning mix
- 1/2 cup water
- 1 cup refried beans
- 1 cup shredded Mexican blend cheese
- 1 cup diced tomatoes
- 1/2 cup diced red onion
- 1/4 cup sliced black olives
- 1/4 cup sliced jalapeños (optional)
- 2 tablespoons chopped fresh cilantro
- 1/2 cup shredded lettuce
- 1/4 cup sour cream
- Hot sauce or salsa for serving (optional)

Instructions:

Preheat the Oven:
- Preheat your oven to the highest temperature it can go, typically around 475-500°F (245-260°C). If you have a pizza stone, place it in the oven to preheat as well.

Prepare the Pizza Dough:
- Dust a work surface with cornmeal or flour. Place the pizza dough on the surface and gently stretch it into a round or rectangular shape, about 12-14 inches in diameter.

Cook the Taco Meat:
- In a skillet, heat olive oil over medium heat. Add ground beef or turkey and cook until browned, breaking it apart with a spoon as it cooks.

- Drain excess fat from the skillet, then stir in taco seasoning mix and water. Simmer for a few minutes until the sauce thickens.

Assemble the Pizza:
- Transfer the stretched pizza dough to a pizza peel or parchment paper-lined baking sheet.
- Spread refried beans evenly over the dough, leaving a small border around the edges.
- Spoon the cooked taco meat evenly over the beans.
- Sprinkle shredded cheese over the taco meat.
- Scatter diced tomatoes, diced red onion, sliced black olives, and sliced jalapeños (if using) over the cheese.

Bake the Pizza:
- If using a pizza stone, carefully transfer the pizza from the peel to the preheated stone in the oven. If using a baking sheet, simply place the baking sheet in the oven.
- Bake the pizza for 10-12 minutes, or until the crust is golden brown and the cheese is melted and bubbly.

Finish and Serve:
- Remove the pizza from the oven and let it cool slightly.
- Scatter shredded lettuce and chopped fresh cilantro over the top of the pizza.
- Drizzle sour cream over the pizza.
- Serve hot, with hot sauce or salsa on the side if desired.

Notes:

- Feel free to customize your taco pizza with additional toppings such as diced avocado, sliced green onions, or shredded cheddar cheese.
- You can use store-bought or homemade pizza dough for this recipe.

Enjoy your delicious homemade taco pizza!

Pesto Chicken Pizza

Ingredients:

For the Pizza Dough:

- 1 pound (about 4 cups) pizza dough, store-bought or homemade
- Cornmeal or flour for dusting

For the Pizza Toppings:

- 1/2 cup basil pesto sauce (store-bought or homemade)
- 1 cup cooked and shredded chicken breast
- 1 cup shredded mozzarella cheese
- 1/4 cup grated Parmesan cheese
- 1/4 cup sliced sun-dried tomatoes
- 1/4 cup sliced black olives
- 2 tablespoons pine nuts (optional)
- Fresh basil leaves, torn, for garnish (optional)
- Crushed red pepper flakes, for serving (optional)

Instructions:

Preheat the Oven:
- Preheat your oven to the highest temperature it can go, typically around 475-500°F (245-260°C). If you have a pizza stone, place it in the oven to preheat as well.

Prepare the Pizza Dough:
- Dust a work surface with cornmeal or flour. Place the pizza dough on the surface and gently stretch it into a round or rectangular shape, about 12-14 inches in diameter.

Assemble the Pizza:
- Transfer the stretched pizza dough to a pizza peel or parchment paper-lined baking sheet.
- Spread basil pesto sauce evenly over the dough, leaving a small border around the edges.
- Scatter cooked and shredded chicken breast evenly over the pesto sauce.
- Sprinkle shredded mozzarella cheese and grated Parmesan cheese evenly over the chicken.
- Distribute sliced sun-dried tomatoes and sliced black olives over the cheese.

- If using pine nuts, sprinkle them over the top of the pizza.

Bake the Pizza:
- If using a pizza stone, carefully transfer the pizza from the peel to the preheated stone in the oven. If using a baking sheet, simply place the baking sheet in the oven.
- Bake the pizza for 10-12 minutes, or until the crust is golden brown and the cheese is melted and bubbly.

Finish and Serve:
- Remove the pizza from the oven and let it cool slightly.
- Garnish with torn fresh basil leaves, if desired.
- Serve hot, optionally with crushed red pepper flakes on the side for added heat.

Notes:

- Feel free to customize your pesto chicken pizza with additional toppings such as sliced cherry tomatoes, caramelized onions, or roasted red peppers.
- You can use store-bought or homemade pizza dough for this recipe.

Enjoy your delicious homemade pesto chicken pizza!

Capricciosa Pizza

Ingredients:

For the Pizza Dough:

- 1 pound (about 4 cups) pizza dough, store-bought or homemade
- Cornmeal or flour for dusting

For the Pizza Toppings:

- 1/2 cup pizza sauce or marinara sauce
- 1 1/2 cups shredded mozzarella cheese
- 4 slices cooked ham, chopped or torn into pieces
- 1/2 cup sliced mushrooms
- 1/4 cup sliced black olives
- 1/4 cup sliced green olives
- 1/4 cup quartered marinated artichoke hearts
- 2 tablespoons grated Parmesan cheese
- 2 tablespoons chopped fresh parsley
- Salt and pepper to taste
- Crushed red pepper flakes (optional)

Instructions:

Preheat the Oven:
- Preheat your oven to the highest temperature it can go, typically around 475-500°F (245-260°C). If you have a pizza stone, place it in the oven to preheat as well.

Prepare the Pizza Dough:
- Dust a work surface with cornmeal or flour. Place the pizza dough on the surface and gently stretch it into a round or rectangular shape, about 12-14 inches in diameter.

Assemble the Pizza:
- Transfer the stretched pizza dough to a pizza peel or parchment paper-lined baking sheet.
- Spread pizza sauce evenly over the dough, leaving a small border around the edges.
- Sprinkle shredded mozzarella cheese evenly over the sauce.

- Distribute chopped or torn cooked ham, sliced mushrooms, sliced black olives, sliced green olives, and quartered marinated artichoke hearts evenly over the cheese.
- Sprinkle grated Parmesan cheese over the top of the pizza.
- Season with salt and pepper to taste.

Bake the Pizza:
- If using a pizza stone, carefully transfer the pizza from the peel to the preheated stone in the oven. If using a baking sheet, simply place the baking sheet in the oven.
- Bake the pizza for 10-12 minutes, or until the crust is golden brown and the cheese is melted and bubbly.

Finish and Serve:
- Remove the pizza from the oven and let it cool slightly.
- Sprinkle chopped fresh parsley over the top of the pizza.
- Optionally, sprinkle crushed red pepper flakes over the pizza for added heat.
- Slice the pizza and serve hot.

Notes:

- Feel free to customize your Capricciosa pizza with additional toppings such as anchovies, roasted red peppers, or caramelized onions.
- You can use store-bought or homemade pizza dough for this recipe.

Enjoy your delicious homemade Capricciosa pizza!

Buffalo Chicken Pizza

Ingredients:

For the Pizza Dough:

- 1 pound (about 4 cups) pizza dough, store-bought or homemade
- Cornmeal or flour for dusting

For the Buffalo Chicken Topping:

- 1 cup cooked and shredded chicken breast
- 1/2 cup buffalo sauce (adjust to taste for desired spiciness)
- 2 tablespoons unsalted butter, melted
- 1/4 cup ranch or blue cheese dressing, plus extra for drizzling
- 1 cup shredded mozzarella cheese
- 1/4 cup crumbled blue cheese (optional)
- 2 tablespoons chopped fresh cilantro or green onions (optional)
- Celery sticks, for serving (optional)

Instructions:

Preheat the Oven:
- Preheat your oven to the highest temperature it can go, typically around 475-500°F (245-260°C). If you have a pizza stone, place it in the oven to preheat as well.

Prepare the Pizza Dough:
- Dust a work surface with cornmeal or flour. Place the pizza dough on the surface and gently stretch it into a round or rectangular shape, about 12-14 inches in diameter.

Prepare the Buffalo Chicken Topping:
- In a bowl, toss the cooked and shredded chicken breast with buffalo sauce until evenly coated.
- In a separate bowl, mix the melted butter with ranch or blue cheese dressing.

Assemble the Pizza:
- Transfer the stretched pizza dough to a pizza peel or parchment paper-lined baking sheet.
- Spread the butter and dressing mixture evenly over the dough, leaving a small border around the edges.

- Scatter the buffalo chicken evenly over the sauce.
- Sprinkle shredded mozzarella cheese over the chicken.
- If using, sprinkle crumbled blue cheese over the top of the pizza.

Bake the Pizza:
- If using a pizza stone, carefully transfer the pizza from the peel to the preheated stone in the oven. If using a baking sheet, simply place the baking sheet in the oven.
- Bake the pizza for 10-12 minutes, or until the crust is golden brown and the cheese is melted and bubbly.

Finish and Serve:
- Remove the pizza from the oven and let it cool slightly.
- Drizzle additional ranch or blue cheese dressing over the top of the pizza.
- If desired, sprinkle chopped fresh cilantro or green onions over the pizza.
- Serve hot, optionally with celery sticks on the side.

Notes:

- Adjust the amount of buffalo sauce to your taste preference for spiciness.
- You can use store-bought or homemade pizza dough for this recipe.

Enjoy your delicious homemade buffalo chicken pizza!

White Pizza with Ricotta and Spinach

Ingredients:

For the Pizza Dough:

- 1 pound (about 4 cups) pizza dough, store-bought or homemade
- Cornmeal or flour for dusting

For the White Pizza Toppings:

- 1 cup ricotta cheese
- 2 cloves garlic, minced
- 1 tablespoon olive oil
- 1/4 teaspoon dried oregano
- 1/4 teaspoon dried basil
- Salt and pepper to taste
- 2 cups fresh spinach leaves
- 1 cup shredded mozzarella cheese
- 1/4 cup grated Parmesan cheese

Instructions:

Preheat the Oven:
- Preheat your oven to the highest temperature it can go, typically around 475-500°F (245-260°C). If you have a pizza stone, place it in the oven to preheat as well.

Prepare the Pizza Dough:
- Dust a work surface with cornmeal or flour. Place the pizza dough on the surface and gently stretch it into a round or rectangular shape, about 12-14 inches in diameter.

Prepare the White Pizza Toppings:
- In a small bowl, mix together the ricotta cheese, minced garlic, olive oil, dried oregano, dried basil, salt, and pepper until well combined.
- Heat a skillet over medium heat and lightly wilt the fresh spinach leaves, about 1-2 minutes. Remove from heat and set aside.

Assemble the Pizza:
- Transfer the stretched pizza dough to a pizza peel or parchment paper-lined baking sheet.

- Spread the ricotta mixture evenly over the dough, leaving a small border around the edges.
- Distribute the wilted spinach evenly over the ricotta mixture.
- Sprinkle shredded mozzarella cheese over the spinach.
- Sprinkle grated Parmesan cheese over the top of the pizza.

Bake the Pizza:
- If using a pizza stone, carefully transfer the pizza from the peel to the preheated stone in the oven. If using a baking sheet, simply place the baking sheet in the oven.
- Bake the pizza for 10-12 minutes, or until the crust is golden brown and the cheese is melted and bubbly.

Finish and Serve:
- Remove the pizza from the oven and let it cool slightly.
- Slice the pizza and serve hot.

Notes:

- Feel free to customize your white pizza with ricotta and spinach by adding additional toppings such as sliced tomatoes, caramelized onions, or roasted garlic.
- You can use store-bought or homemade pizza dough for this recipe.

Enjoy your delicious homemade white pizza with ricotta and spinach!

Sausage and Peppers Pizza

Ingredients:

For the Pizza Dough:

- 1 pound (about 4 cups) pizza dough, store-bought or homemade
- Cornmeal or flour for dusting

For the Pizza Toppings:

- 1/2 cup pizza sauce or marinara sauce
- 1 1/2 cups shredded mozzarella cheese
- 4 Italian sausages, cooked and sliced into rounds
- 1 bell pepper, thinly sliced
- 1 onion, thinly sliced
- 2 cloves garlic, minced
- 2 tablespoons olive oil
- Salt and pepper to taste
- Crushed red pepper flakes (optional)
- Grated Parmesan cheese for serving (optional)

Instructions:

Preheat the Oven:
- Preheat your oven to the highest temperature it can go, typically around 475-500°F (245-260°C). If you have a pizza stone, place it in the oven to preheat as well.

Prepare the Pizza Dough:
- Dust a work surface with cornmeal or flour. Place the pizza dough on the surface and gently stretch it into a round or rectangular shape, about 12-14 inches in diameter.

Cook the Sausage and Peppers:
- In a skillet, heat olive oil over medium heat. Add sliced Italian sausages, bell pepper, onion, and minced garlic to the skillet.
- Cook, stirring occasionally, until the sausage is browned and the peppers and onions are softened, about 8-10 minutes. Season with salt and pepper to taste.

Assemble the Pizza:

- Transfer the stretched pizza dough to a pizza peel or parchment paper-lined baking sheet.
- Spread pizza sauce evenly over the dough, leaving a small border around the edges.
- Sprinkle shredded mozzarella cheese evenly over the sauce.
- Distribute the cooked sausage and peppers mixture evenly over the cheese.

Bake the Pizza:
- If using a pizza stone, carefully transfer the pizza from the peel to the preheated stone in the oven. If using a baking sheet, simply place the baking sheet in the oven.
- Bake the pizza for 10-12 minutes, or until the crust is golden brown and the cheese is melted and bubbly.

Finish and Serve:
- Remove the pizza from the oven and let it cool slightly.
- Optionally, sprinkle crushed red pepper flakes over the pizza for added heat.
- Serve hot, optionally with grated Parmesan cheese on top.

Notes:

- Feel free to customize your sausage and peppers pizza with additional toppings such as sliced mushrooms or black olives.
- You can use store-bought or homemade pizza dough for this recipe.

Enjoy your delicious homemade sausage and peppers pizza!

Chicken Alfredo Pizza

Ingredients:

For the Pizza Dough:

- 1 pound (about 4 cups) pizza dough, store-bought or homemade
- Cornmeal or flour for dusting

For the Alfredo Sauce:

- 2 tablespoons unsalted butter
- 2 cloves garlic, minced
- 2 tablespoons all-purpose flour
- 1 cup heavy cream
- 1/2 cup grated Parmesan cheese
- Salt and pepper to taste

For the Pizza Toppings:

- 1 cup cooked and shredded chicken breast
- 1 cup shredded mozzarella cheese
- 1/4 cup grated Parmesan cheese
- 2 tablespoons chopped fresh parsley
- Salt and pepper to taste
- Red pepper flakes (optional)
- Olive oil for brushing

Instructions:

Preheat the Oven:
- Preheat your oven to the highest temperature it can go, typically around 475-500°F (245-260°C). If you have a pizza stone, place it in the oven to preheat as well.

Prepare the Pizza Dough:
- Dust a work surface with cornmeal or flour. Place the pizza dough on the surface and gently stretch it into a round or rectangular shape, about 12-14 inches in diameter.

Make the Alfredo Sauce:
- In a saucepan, melt the butter over medium heat. Add minced garlic and cook until fragrant, about 1 minute.
- Stir in the flour and cook for another minute, stirring constantly.

- Slowly pour in the heavy cream, whisking constantly to prevent lumps from forming.
- Cook the sauce, stirring frequently, until it thickens, about 3-5 minutes.
- Remove the saucepan from the heat and stir in the grated Parmesan cheese until melted and smooth. Season with salt and pepper to taste.

Assemble the Pizza:
- Transfer the stretched pizza dough to a pizza peel or parchment paper-lined baking sheet.
- Brush the crust with olive oil.
- Spread the Alfredo sauce evenly over the dough, leaving a small border around the edges.
- Scatter cooked and shredded chicken breast evenly over the sauce.
- Sprinkle shredded mozzarella cheese and grated Parmesan cheese over the chicken.
- Season with salt and pepper to taste.

Bake the Pizza:
- If using a pizza stone, carefully transfer the pizza from the peel to the preheated stone in the oven. If using a baking sheet, simply place the baking sheet in the oven.
- Bake the pizza for 10-12 minutes, or until the crust is golden brown and the cheese is melted and bubbly.

Finish and Serve:
- Remove the pizza from the oven and let it cool slightly.
- Sprinkle chopped fresh parsley and red pepper flakes (if using) over the top of the pizza.
- Slice the pizza and serve hot.

Notes:

- Feel free to customize your Chicken Alfredo pizza with additional toppings such as sliced mushrooms, cooked bacon, or spinach.
- You can use store-bought or homemade pizza dough for this recipe.

Enjoy your delicious homemade Chicken Alfredo pizza!

Shrimp Scampi Pizza

Ingredients:

For the Pizza Dough:

- 1 pound (about 4 cups) pizza dough, store-bought or homemade
- Cornmeal or flour for dusting

For the Shrimp Scampi Topping:

- 1 pound large shrimp, peeled and deveined
- 4 cloves garlic, minced
- 2 tablespoons unsalted butter
- 2 tablespoons olive oil
- 1/4 cup dry white wine (optional)
- Zest of 1 lemon
- Juice of 1 lemon
- Salt and pepper to taste
- Crushed red pepper flakes (optional)
- 1/4 cup chopped fresh parsley

For the Pizza Assembly:

- 1 cup shredded mozzarella cheese
- 1/4 cup grated Parmesan cheese
- 2 tablespoons chopped fresh parsley
- Lemon wedges, for serving

Instructions:

Preheat the Oven:
- Preheat your oven to the highest temperature it can go, typically around 475-500°F (245-260°C). If you have a pizza stone, place it in the oven to preheat as well.

Prepare the Shrimp Scampi Topping:
- In a skillet, heat olive oil and butter over medium heat. Add minced garlic and sauté for about 1 minute, until fragrant.
- Add the shrimp to the skillet and cook until they turn pink, about 2-3 minutes per side.

- Pour in the white wine (if using) and cook for another 2 minutes, until the alcohol evaporates.
- Stir in the lemon zest and juice. Season with salt, pepper, and crushed red pepper flakes (if using). Remove from heat and stir in chopped parsley.

Assemble the Pizza:
- Transfer the stretched pizza dough to a pizza peel or parchment paper-lined baking sheet.
- Spread shredded mozzarella cheese evenly over the dough, leaving a small border around the edges.
- Arrange the cooked shrimp scampi mixture evenly over the cheese.
- Sprinkle grated Parmesan cheese over the top of the pizza.
- If desired, sprinkle additional chopped parsley over the pizza.

Bake the Pizza:
- If using a pizza stone, carefully transfer the pizza from the peel to the preheated stone in the oven. If using a baking sheet, simply place the baking sheet in the oven.
- Bake the pizza for 10-12 minutes, or until the crust is golden brown and the cheese is melted and bubbly.

Finish and Serve:
- Remove the pizza from the oven and let it cool slightly.
- Serve hot, with lemon wedges on the side for squeezing over the pizza.

Notes:

- Feel free to customize your shrimp scampi pizza with additional toppings such as sliced cherry tomatoes or chopped green onions.
- You can use store-bought or homemade pizza dough for this recipe.

Enjoy your delicious homemade shrimp scampi pizza!

Greek Pizza

Ingredients:

For the Pizza Dough:

- 1 pound (about 4 cups) pizza dough, store-bought or homemade
- Cornmeal or flour for dusting

For the Pizza Toppings:

- 1/2 cup pizza sauce or marinara sauce
- 1 1/2 cups shredded mozzarella cheese
- 1/2 cup crumbled feta cheese
- 1/4 cup sliced black olives
- 1/4 cup sliced Kalamata olives
- 1/4 cup sliced red onion
- 1/2 cup sliced cherry tomatoes
- 1 tablespoon chopped fresh oregano (or 1 teaspoon dried oregano)
- 1 tablespoon extra virgin olive oil
- Salt and pepper to taste

Instructions:

Preheat the Oven:
- Preheat your oven to the highest temperature it can go, typically around 475-500°F (245-260°C). If you have a pizza stone, place it in the oven to preheat as well.

Prepare the Pizza Dough:
- Dust a work surface with cornmeal or flour. Place the pizza dough on the surface and gently stretch it into a round or rectangular shape, about 12-14 inches in diameter.

Assemble the Pizza:
- Transfer the stretched pizza dough to a pizza peel or parchment paper-lined baking sheet.
- Spread pizza sauce evenly over the dough, leaving a small border around the edges.
- Sprinkle shredded mozzarella cheese evenly over the sauce.
- Scatter crumbled feta cheese, sliced black olives, sliced Kalamata olives, sliced red onion, and sliced cherry tomatoes over the cheese.

- Sprinkle chopped fresh oregano over the top of the pizza.
- Drizzle extra virgin olive oil over the toppings. Season with salt and pepper to taste.

Bake the Pizza:
- If using a pizza stone, carefully transfer the pizza from the peel to the preheated stone in the oven. If using a baking sheet, simply place the baking sheet in the oven.
- Bake the pizza for 10-12 minutes, or until the crust is golden brown and the cheese is melted and bubbly.

Finish and Serve:
- Remove the pizza from the oven and let it cool slightly.
- Slice the pizza and serve hot.

Notes:

- Feel free to customize your Greek pizza with additional toppings such as artichoke hearts, roasted red peppers, or capers.
- You can use store-bought or homemade pizza dough for this recipe.

Enjoy your delicious homemade Greek pizza!

Artichoke and Olive Pizza

Ingredients:

For the Pizza Dough:

- 1 pound (about 4 cups) pizza dough, store-bought or homemade
- Cornmeal or flour for dusting

For the Pizza Toppings:

- 1/2 cup pizza sauce or marinara sauce
- 1 1/2 cups shredded mozzarella cheese
- 1/2 cup marinated artichoke hearts, drained and chopped
- 1/4 cup sliced black olives
- 1/4 cup sliced Kalamata olives
- 1/4 cup sliced red onion
- 1 tablespoon chopped fresh parsley
- 1 tablespoon extra virgin olive oil
- Salt and pepper to taste

Instructions:

Preheat the Oven:
- Preheat your oven to the highest temperature it can go, typically around 475-500°F (245-260°C). If you have a pizza stone, place it in the oven to preheat as well.

Prepare the Pizza Dough:
- Dust a work surface with cornmeal or flour. Place the pizza dough on the surface and gently stretch it into a round or rectangular shape, about 12-14 inches in diameter.

Assemble the Pizza:
- Transfer the stretched pizza dough to a pizza peel or parchment paper-lined baking sheet.
- Spread pizza sauce evenly over the dough, leaving a small border around the edges.
- Sprinkle shredded mozzarella cheese evenly over the sauce.
- Scatter chopped marinated artichoke hearts, sliced black olives, sliced Kalamata olives, and sliced red onion over the cheese.
- Drizzle extra virgin olive oil over the toppings. Season with salt and pepper to taste.

Bake the Pizza:
- If using a pizza stone, carefully transfer the pizza from the peel to the preheated stone in the oven. If using a baking sheet, simply place the baking sheet in the oven.
- Bake the pizza for 10-12 minutes, or until the crust is golden brown and the cheese is melted and bubbly.

Finish and Serve:
- Remove the pizza from the oven and let it cool slightly.
- Sprinkle chopped fresh parsley over the top of the pizza.
- Slice the pizza and serve hot.

Notes:

- Feel free to customize your artichoke and olive pizza with additional toppings such as roasted red peppers, sun-dried tomatoes, or capers.
- You can use store-bought or homemade pizza dough for this recipe.

Enjoy your delicious homemade artichoke and olive pizza!

Roasted Vegetable Pizza

Ingredients:

For the Pizza Dough:

- 1 pound (about 4 cups) pizza dough, store-bought or homemade
- Cornmeal or flour for dusting

For the Roasted Vegetables:

- 1 medium eggplant, sliced into 1/4-inch rounds
- 1 medium zucchini, sliced into 1/4-inch rounds
- 1 red bell pepper, sliced into thin strips
- 1 yellow bell pepper, sliced into thin strips
- 1 red onion, thinly sliced
- 2 tablespoons olive oil
- Salt and pepper to taste
- 2 cloves garlic, minced
- 1 tablespoon chopped fresh herbs (such as rosemary, thyme, or oregano)

For the Pizza Toppings:

- 1/2 cup pizza sauce or marinara sauce
- 1 1/2 cups shredded mozzarella cheese
- 1/4 cup grated Parmesan cheese
- Red pepper flakes (optional)
- Fresh basil leaves, torn, for garnish (optional)

Instructions:

  Preheat the Oven:
  - Preheat your oven to 425°F (220°C). Line a baking sheet with parchment paper.

  Prepare the Roasted Vegetables:
  - In a large bowl, toss the sliced eggplant, zucchini, bell peppers, and red onion with olive oil, salt, pepper, minced garlic, and chopped fresh herbs until evenly coated.
  - Spread the vegetables in a single layer on the prepared baking sheet.
  - Roast in the preheated oven for 20-25 minutes, or until the vegetables are tender and lightly browned, stirring halfway through.

Prepare the Pizza Dough:
- Dust a work surface with cornmeal or flour. Place the pizza dough on the surface and gently stretch it into a round or rectangular shape, about 12-14 inches in diameter.

Assemble the Pizza:
- Transfer the stretched pizza dough to a pizza peel or parchment paper-lined baking sheet.
- Spread pizza sauce evenly over the dough, leaving a small border around the edges.
- Sprinkle shredded mozzarella cheese evenly over the sauce.
- Arrange the roasted vegetables evenly over the cheese.
- Sprinkle grated Parmesan cheese over the top of the pizza. If desired, add red pepper flakes for extra heat.

Bake the Pizza:
- If using a pizza stone, carefully transfer the pizza from the peel to the preheated stone in the oven. If using a baking sheet, simply place the baking sheet in the oven.
- Bake the pizza for 12-15 minutes, or until the crust is golden brown and the cheese is melted and bubbly.

Finish and Serve:
- Remove the pizza from the oven and let it cool slightly.
- Garnish with torn fresh basil leaves, if desired.
- Slice the pizza and serve hot.

Notes:

- Feel free to customize your roasted vegetable pizza with additional toppings such as sliced mushrooms, cherry tomatoes, or olives.
- You can use store-bought or homemade pizza dough for this recipe.

Enjoy your delicious homemade roasted vegetable pizza!

Smoked Salmon Pizza

Ingredients:

For the Pizza Dough:

- 1 pound (about 4 cups) pizza dough, store-bought or homemade
- Cornmeal or flour for dusting

For the Pizza Toppings:

- 1/2 cup crème fraîche or sour cream
- 1 tablespoon chopped fresh dill
- 1 tablespoon capers, drained
- 1/4 red onion, thinly sliced
- 4 ounces smoked salmon, thinly sliced
- 1 tablespoon lemon zest
- Freshly ground black pepper, to taste
- Arugula or microgreens, for garnish (optional)

Instructions:

Preheat the Oven:
- Preheat your oven to the highest temperature it can go, typically around 475-500°F (245-260°C). If you have a pizza stone, place it in the oven to preheat as well.

Prepare the Pizza Dough:
- Dust a work surface with cornmeal or flour. Place the pizza dough on the surface and gently stretch it into a round or rectangular shape, about 12-14 inches in diameter.

Assemble the Pizza:
- Transfer the stretched pizza dough to a pizza peel or parchment paper-lined baking sheet.
- In a small bowl, mix the crème fraîche or sour cream with chopped fresh dill.
- Spread the crème fraîche mixture evenly over the dough, leaving a small border around the edges.
- Scatter capers and thinly sliced red onion over the crème fraîche mixture.
- Arrange the smoked salmon slices on top of the pizza.
- Sprinkle lemon zest evenly over the smoked salmon.
- Season with freshly ground black pepper to taste.

Bake the Pizza:
- If using a pizza stone, carefully transfer the pizza from the peel to the preheated stone in the oven. If using a baking sheet, simply place the baking sheet in the oven.
- Bake the pizza for 10-12 minutes, or until the crust is golden brown and the toppings are heated through.

Finish and Serve:
- Remove the pizza from the oven and let it cool slightly.
- Garnish with arugula or microgreens, if desired.
- Slice the pizza and serve hot.

Notes:

- Feel free to customize your smoked salmon pizza with additional toppings such as thinly sliced cucumber or avocado.
- You can use store-bought or homemade pizza dough for this recipe.

Enjoy your delicious homemade smoked salmon pizza!

Fig and Goat Cheese Pizza

Ingredients:

For the Pizza Dough:

- 1 pound (about 4 cups) pizza dough, store-bought or homemade
- Cornmeal or flour for dusting

For the Pizza Toppings:

- 1/2 cup fig jam or preserves
- 4 ounces goat cheese, crumbled
- 6-8 fresh figs, thinly sliced
- 2 tablespoons honey
- Fresh thyme leaves, for garnish
- Balsamic glaze, for drizzling (optional)
- Salt and pepper to taste

Instructions:

Preheat the Oven:
- Preheat your oven to the highest temperature it can go, typically around 475-500°F (245-260°C). If you have a pizza stone, place it in the oven to preheat as well.

Prepare the Pizza Dough:
- Dust a work surface with cornmeal or flour. Place the pizza dough on the surface and gently stretch it into a round or rectangular shape, about 12-14 inches in diameter.

Assemble the Pizza:
- Transfer the stretched pizza dough to a pizza peel or parchment paper-lined baking sheet.
- Spread fig jam or preserves evenly over the dough, leaving a small border around the edges.
- Scatter crumbled goat cheese over the fig jam.
- Arrange the thinly sliced fresh figs on top of the pizza.
- Drizzle honey evenly over the figs.
- Season lightly with salt and pepper.

Bake the Pizza:

- If using a pizza stone, carefully transfer the pizza from the peel to the preheated stone in the oven. If using a baking sheet, simply place the baking sheet in the oven.
- Bake the pizza for 10-12 minutes, or until the crust is golden brown and the toppings are heated through.

Finish and Serve:
- Remove the pizza from the oven and let it cool slightly.
- Garnish with fresh thyme leaves.
- Optionally, drizzle balsamic glaze over the pizza for extra flavor.
- Slice the pizza and serve hot.

Notes:

- Feel free to customize your fig and goat cheese pizza with additional toppings such as prosciutto, arugula, or caramelized onions.
- You can use store-bought or homemade pizza dough for this recipe.

Enjoy your delicious homemade fig and goat cheese pizza!

Blue Cheese and Pear Pizza

Ingredients:

For the Pizza Dough:

- 1 pound (about 4 cups) pizza dough, store-bought or homemade
- Cornmeal or flour for dusting

For the Pizza Toppings:

- 1/2 cup crumbled blue cheese (such as Gorgonzola or Roquefort)
- 1 large ripe pear, thinly sliced
- 1/4 cup chopped walnuts or pecans
- 1 tablespoon honey
- 1 tablespoon balsamic glaze (optional)
- Fresh thyme leaves, for garnish
- Salt and pepper to taste

Instructions:

Preheat the Oven:
- Preheat your oven to the highest temperature it can go, typically around 475-500°F (245-260°C). If you have a pizza stone, place it in the oven to preheat as well.

Prepare the Pizza Dough:
- Dust a work surface with cornmeal or flour. Place the pizza dough on the surface and gently stretch it into a round or rectangular shape, about 12-14 inches in diameter.

Assemble the Pizza:
- Transfer the stretched pizza dough to a pizza peel or parchment paper-lined baking sheet.
- Scatter crumbled blue cheese evenly over the dough, leaving a small border around the edges.
- Arrange the thinly sliced pear on top of the blue cheese.
- Sprinkle chopped walnuts or pecans over the pear slices.
- Drizzle honey evenly over the pizza.
- Season lightly with salt and pepper.

Bake the Pizza:

- If using a pizza stone, carefully transfer the pizza from the peel to the preheated stone in the oven. If using a baking sheet, simply place the baking sheet in the oven.
- Bake the pizza for 10-12 minutes, or until the crust is golden brown and the toppings are heated through.

Finish and Serve:
- Remove the pizza from the oven and let it cool slightly.
- Optionally, drizzle balsamic glaze over the pizza for extra flavor.
- Garnish with fresh thyme leaves.
- Slice the pizza and serve hot.

Notes:

- Feel free to customize your blue cheese and pear pizza with additional toppings such as caramelized onions, arugula, or prosciutto.
- You can use store-bought or homemade pizza dough for this recipe.

Enjoy your delicious homemade blue cheese and pear pizza!

Margherita with Balsamic Glaze Pizza

Ingredients:

For the Pizza Dough:

- 1 pound (about 4 cups) pizza dough, store-bought or homemade
- Cornmeal or flour for dusting

For the Pizza Toppings:

- 1/2 cup pizza sauce or marinara sauce
- 8 ounces fresh mozzarella cheese, thinly sliced
- 2 large ripe tomatoes, thinly sliced
- Fresh basil leaves
- Salt and pepper to taste
- Balsamic glaze, for drizzling
- Extra virgin olive oil, for drizzling

Instructions:

Preheat the Oven:
- Preheat your oven to the highest temperature it can go, typically around 475-500°F (245-260°C). If you have a pizza stone, place it in the oven to preheat as well.

Prepare the Pizza Dough:
- Dust a work surface with cornmeal or flour. Place the pizza dough on the surface and gently stretch it into a round or rectangular shape, about 12-14 inches in diameter.

Assemble the Pizza:
- Transfer the stretched pizza dough to a pizza peel or parchment paper-lined baking sheet.
- Spread pizza sauce evenly over the dough, leaving a small border around the edges.
- Arrange the thinly sliced fresh mozzarella cheese evenly over the sauce.
- Place the thinly sliced tomatoes on top of the cheese.
- Season with salt and pepper to taste.
- Tear fresh basil leaves and scatter them over the pizza.

Bake the Pizza:

- If using a pizza stone, carefully transfer the pizza from the peel to the preheated stone in the oven. If using a baking sheet, simply place the baking sheet in the oven.
- Bake the pizza for 10-12 minutes, or until the crust is golden brown and the cheese is melted and bubbly.

Finish and Serve:
- Remove the pizza from the oven and let it cool slightly.
- Drizzle balsamic glaze and extra virgin olive oil over the pizza.
- Slice the pizza and serve hot.

Notes:

- You can make balsamic glaze by simmering balsamic vinegar over low heat until it thickens, or you can use store-bought balsamic glaze.
- Feel free to add extra toppings such as garlic, olives, or red pepper flakes according to your preference.
- You can use store-bought or homemade pizza dough for this recipe.

Enjoy your delicious homemade Margherita with balsamic glaze pizza!

Potato and Rosemary Pizza

Ingredients:

For the Pizza Dough:

- 1 pound (about 4 cups) pizza dough, store-bought or homemade
- Cornmeal or flour for dusting

For the Pizza Toppings:

- 2 medium-sized potatoes, peeled and thinly sliced
- 2 tablespoons olive oil
- 2 cloves garlic, minced
- 1 tablespoon fresh rosemary leaves, chopped
- Salt and pepper to taste
- 1 1/2 cups shredded mozzarella cheese
- 1/4 cup grated Parmesan cheese
- Red pepper flakes (optional)
- Fresh arugula, for garnish (optional)

Instructions:

Preheat the Oven:
- Preheat your oven to the highest temperature it can go, typically around 475-500°F (245-260°C). If you have a pizza stone, place it in the oven to preheat as well.

Prepare the Pizza Dough:
- Dust a work surface with cornmeal or flour. Place the pizza dough on the surface and gently stretch it into a round or rectangular shape, about 12-14 inches in diameter.

Prepare the Potato Toppings:
- In a skillet, heat olive oil over medium heat. Add minced garlic and chopped rosemary leaves. Cook for about 1 minute until fragrant.
- Add the thinly sliced potatoes to the skillet. Season with salt and pepper to taste. Cook, stirring occasionally, until the potatoes are tender, about 8-10 minutes. Remove from heat and set aside.

Assemble the Pizza:
- Transfer the stretched pizza dough to a pizza peel or parchment paper-lined baking sheet.

- Spread shredded mozzarella cheese evenly over the dough, leaving a small border around the edges.
- Arrange the cooked potato slices evenly over the cheese.
- Sprinkle grated Parmesan cheese over the top of the pizza.
- Optionally, sprinkle red pepper flakes over the pizza for extra heat.

Bake the Pizza:

- If using a pizza stone, carefully transfer the pizza from the peel to the preheated stone in the oven. If using a baking sheet, simply place the baking sheet in the oven.
- Bake the pizza for 10-12 minutes, or until the crust is golden brown and the cheese is melted and bubbly.

Finish and Serve:

- Remove the pizza from the oven and let it cool slightly.
- Garnish with fresh arugula, if desired.
- Slice the pizza and serve hot.

Notes:

- Feel free to customize your potato and rosemary pizza with additional toppings such as caramelized onions or crispy bacon.
- You can use store-bought or homemade pizza dough for this recipe.

Enjoy your delicious homemade potato and rosemary pizza!

Pumpkin and Sage Pizza

Ingredients:

For the Pizza Dough:

- 1 pound (about 4 cups) pizza dough, store-bought or homemade
- Cornmeal or flour for dusting

For the Pizza Toppings:

- 1 cup pumpkin puree
- 2 tablespoons olive oil
- 2 cloves garlic, minced
- 1 tablespoon chopped fresh sage leaves
- Salt and pepper to taste
- 1 1/2 cups shredded mozzarella cheese
- 1/4 cup grated Parmesan cheese
- Red pepper flakes (optional)
- Fresh arugula, for garnish (optional)

Instructions:

Preheat the Oven:
- Preheat your oven to the highest temperature it can go, typically around 475-500°F (245-260°C). If you have a pizza stone, place it in the oven to preheat as well.

Prepare the Pizza Dough:
- Dust a work surface with cornmeal or flour. Place the pizza dough on the surface and gently stretch it into a round or rectangular shape, about 12-14 inches in diameter.

Prepare the Pumpkin Topping:
- In a small bowl, mix together the pumpkin puree, olive oil, minced garlic, chopped sage leaves, salt, and pepper until well combined.

Assemble the Pizza:
- Transfer the stretched pizza dough to a pizza peel or parchment paper-lined baking sheet.
- Spread the pumpkin mixture evenly over the dough, leaving a small border around the edges.
- Sprinkle shredded mozzarella cheese evenly over the pumpkin mixture.
- Sprinkle grated Parmesan cheese over the top of the pizza.

- Optionally, sprinkle red pepper flakes over the pizza for extra heat.

Bake the Pizza:
- If using a pizza stone, carefully transfer the pizza from the peel to the preheated stone in the oven. If using a baking sheet, simply place the baking sheet in the oven.
- Bake the pizza for 10-12 minutes, or until the crust is golden brown and the cheese is melted and bubbly.

Finish and Serve:
- Remove the pizza from the oven and let it cool slightly.
- Garnish with fresh arugula, if desired.
- Slice the pizza and serve hot.

Notes:

- Feel free to customize your pumpkin and sage pizza with additional toppings such as caramelized onions or crispy bacon.
- You can use store-bought or homemade pizza dough for this recipe.

Enjoy your delicious homemade pumpkin and sage pizza!

Beef and Blue Cheese Pizza

Ingredients:

For the Pizza Dough:

- 1 pound (about 4 cups) pizza dough, store-bought or homemade
- Cornmeal or flour for dusting

For the Pizza Toppings:

- 1/2 pound beef sirloin or flank steak, thinly sliced
- 2 tablespoons olive oil
- 2 cloves garlic, minced
- Salt and pepper to taste
- 1 cup crumbled blue cheese (such as Gorgonzola or Roquefort)
- 1/2 cup shredded mozzarella cheese
- 1/4 cup grated Parmesan cheese
- 1/4 cup chopped fresh parsley
- Red pepper flakes (optional)

Instructions:

Preheat the Oven:
- Preheat your oven to the highest temperature it can go, typically around 475-500°F (245-260°C). If you have a pizza stone, place it in the oven to preheat as well.

Prepare the Pizza Dough:
- Dust a work surface with cornmeal or flour. Place the pizza dough on the surface and gently stretch it into a round or rectangular shape, about 12-14 inches in diameter.

Prepare the Beef Topping:
- In a skillet, heat olive oil over medium-high heat. Add minced garlic and sauté for about 1 minute until fragrant.
- Add the thinly sliced beef to the skillet. Season with salt and pepper to taste. Cook, stirring occasionally, until the beef is browned and cooked to your desired doneness, about 3-4 minutes. Remove from heat and set aside.

Assemble the Pizza:
- Transfer the stretched pizza dough to a pizza peel or parchment paper-lined baking sheet.

- Spread shredded mozzarella cheese evenly over the dough, leaving a small border around the edges.
- Scatter cooked beef evenly over the cheese.
- Sprinkle crumbled blue cheese and grated Parmesan cheese over the beef.
- Optionally, sprinkle chopped fresh parsley and red pepper flakes over the pizza for extra flavor.

Bake the Pizza:
- If using a pizza stone, carefully transfer the pizza from the peel to the preheated stone in the oven. If using a baking sheet, simply place the baking sheet in the oven.
- Bake the pizza for 10-12 minutes, or until the crust is golden brown and the cheese is melted and bubbly.

Finish and Serve:
- Remove the pizza from the oven and let it cool slightly.
- Slice the pizza and serve hot.

Notes:

- Feel free to customize your beef and blue cheese pizza with additional toppings such as caramelized onions or sautéed mushrooms.
- You can use store-bought or homemade pizza dough for this recipe.

Enjoy your delicious homemade beef and blue cheese pizza!

Reindeer Sausage Pizza

Ingredients:

For the Pizza Dough:

- 1 pound (about 4 cups) pizza dough, store-bought or homemade
- Cornmeal or flour for dusting

For the Pizza Toppings:

- 1/2 pound reindeer sausage, thinly sliced
- 1 tablespoon olive oil
- 1/2 small red onion, thinly sliced
- 1 cup shredded mozzarella cheese
- 1/4 cup grated Parmesan cheese
- 1/4 cup chopped fresh parsley
- Red pepper flakes (optional)
- Salt and pepper to taste

Instructions:

Preheat the Oven:
- Preheat your oven to the highest temperature it can go, typically around 475-500°F (245-260°C). If you have a pizza stone, place it in the oven to preheat as well.

Prepare the Pizza Dough:
- Dust a work surface with cornmeal or flour. Place the pizza dough on the surface and gently stretch it into a round or rectangular shape, about 12-14 inches in diameter.

Prepare the Reindeer Sausage:
- In a skillet, heat olive oil over medium-high heat. Add thinly sliced reindeer sausage and cook until browned and cooked through, about 5-6 minutes. Remove from heat and set aside.

Assemble the Pizza:
- Transfer the stretched pizza dough to a pizza peel or parchment paper-lined baking sheet.
- Spread shredded mozzarella cheese evenly over the dough, leaving a small border around the edges.
- Scatter cooked reindeer sausage evenly over the cheese.
- Arrange thinly sliced red onion over the sausage.

- Sprinkle grated Parmesan cheese over the top of the pizza.
- Optionally, sprinkle chopped fresh parsley and red pepper flakes over the pizza for extra flavor.

Bake the Pizza:
- If using a pizza stone, carefully transfer the pizza from the peel to the preheated stone in the oven. If using a baking sheet, simply place the baking sheet in the oven.
- Bake the pizza for 10-12 minutes, or until the crust is golden brown and the cheese is melted and bubbly.

Finish and Serve:
- Remove the pizza from the oven and let it cool slightly.
- Slice the pizza and serve hot.

Notes:

- Reindeer sausage is a specialty ingredient that may not be readily available everywhere. You can substitute it with other types of sausage, such as Italian sausage or bratwurst.
- Feel free to customize your reindeer sausage pizza with additional toppings such as bell peppers or mushrooms.
- You can use store-bought or homemade pizza dough for this recipe.

Enjoy your delicious homemade reindeer sausage pizza!

Clam and Garlic Pizza

Ingredients:

For the Pizza Dough:

- 1 pound (about 4 cups) pizza dough, store-bought or homemade
- Cornmeal or flour for dusting

For the Pizza Toppings:

- 1 can (6.5 ounces) chopped clams, drained
- 2 tablespoons olive oil
- 4 cloves garlic, thinly sliced
- 1/2 cup shredded mozzarella cheese
- 1/4 cup grated Parmesan cheese
- Red pepper flakes (optional)
- Fresh parsley, chopped, for garnish
- Lemon wedges, for serving

Instructions:

Preheat the Oven:
- Preheat your oven to the highest temperature it can go, typically around 475-500°F (245-260°C). If you have a pizza stone, place it in the oven to preheat as well.

Prepare the Pizza Dough:
- Dust a work surface with cornmeal or flour. Place the pizza dough on the surface and gently stretch it into a round or rectangular shape, about 12-14 inches in diameter.

Prepare the Clam Topping:
- In a small skillet, heat olive oil over medium heat. Add thinly sliced garlic and sauté until fragrant and lightly golden, about 1-2 minutes. Be careful not to burn the garlic.
- Add the drained chopped clams to the skillet and cook for an additional 1-2 minutes, stirring occasionally. Remove from heat and set aside.

Assemble the Pizza:
- Transfer the stretched pizza dough to a pizza peel or parchment paper-lined baking sheet.
- Spread shredded mozzarella cheese evenly over the dough, leaving a small border around the edges.

- Spoon the cooked clam and garlic mixture evenly over the cheese.
- Sprinkle grated Parmesan cheese over the top of the pizza.
- Optionally, sprinkle red pepper flakes over the pizza for extra heat.

Bake the Pizza:
- If using a pizza stone, carefully transfer the pizza from the peel to the preheated stone in the oven. If using a baking sheet, simply place the baking sheet in the oven.
- Bake the pizza for 10-12 minutes, or until the crust is golden brown and the cheese is melted and bubbly.

Finish and Serve:
- Remove the pizza from the oven and let it cool slightly.
- Garnish with chopped fresh parsley.
- Serve hot with lemon wedges on the side.

Notes:

- Feel free to add additional toppings such as chopped fresh herbs, diced tomatoes, or thinly sliced onions to customize your clam and garlic pizza.
- You can use store-bought or homemade pizza dough for this recipe.

Enjoy your delicious homemade clam and garlic pizza!

Chicken Tikka Masala Pizza

Ingredients:

For the Pizza Dough:

- 1 pound (about 4 cups) pizza dough, store-bought or homemade
- Cornmeal or flour for dusting

For the Chicken Tikka Masala Topping:

- 1 cup cooked chicken tikka masala, chopped into bite-sized pieces
- 1/2 cup diced tomatoes
- 1/4 cup diced red onions
- 1/4 cup chopped cilantro (coriander leaves)
- 1 cup shredded mozzarella cheese
- 1/4 cup crumbled paneer cheese (optional)
- Red pepper flakes (optional)

For the Garnish:

- Fresh cilantro leaves
- Lime wedges
- Mango chutney or mint chutney (optional)

Instructions:

Preheat the Oven:
- Preheat your oven to the highest temperature it can go, typically around 475-500°F (245-260°C). If you have a pizza stone, place it in the oven to preheat as well.

Prepare the Pizza Dough:
- Dust a work surface with cornmeal or flour. Place the pizza dough on the surface and gently stretch it into a round or rectangular shape, about 12-14 inches in diameter.

Assemble the Pizza:
- Transfer the stretched pizza dough to a pizza peel or parchment paper-lined baking sheet.
- Spread the cooked chicken tikka masala evenly over the dough, leaving a small border around the edges.
- Sprinkle diced tomatoes and red onions over the chicken tikka masala.

- Scatter chopped cilantro over the top.
- Sprinkle shredded mozzarella cheese evenly over the pizza.
- Optionally, sprinkle crumbled paneer cheese and red pepper flakes over the pizza for extra flavor.

Bake the Pizza:
- If using a pizza stone, carefully transfer the pizza from the peel to the preheated stone in the oven. If using a baking sheet, simply place the baking sheet in the oven.
- Bake the pizza for 10-12 minutes, or until the crust is golden brown and the cheese is melted and bubbly.

Finish and Serve:
- Remove the pizza from the oven and let it cool slightly.
- Garnish with fresh cilantro leaves.
- Serve hot with lime wedges and mango chutney or mint chutney on the side, if desired.

Notes:

- Feel free to customize your chicken tikka masala pizza with additional toppings such as sliced green bell peppers, diced red bell peppers, or sliced jalapeños.
- You can use store-bought or homemade pizza dough for this recipe.

Enjoy your delicious homemade chicken tikka masala pizza!

Apple and Cheddar Pizza

Ingredients:

For the Pizza Dough:

- 1 pound (about 4 cups) pizza dough, store-bought or homemade
- Cornmeal or flour for dusting

For the Pizza Toppings:

- 1 large apple, thinly sliced (such as Granny Smith or Honeycrisp)
- 1 tablespoon lemon juice (to prevent browning)
- 1 tablespoon olive oil
- 1/2 teaspoon ground cinnamon
- 1 1/2 cups shredded sharp cheddar cheese
- 2 tablespoons honey
- 2 tablespoons chopped fresh thyme leaves
- Salt and pepper to taste

Instructions:

Preheat the Oven:
- Preheat your oven to the highest temperature it can go, typically around 475-500°F (245-260°C). If you have a pizza stone, place it in the oven to preheat as well.

Prepare the Pizza Dough:
- Dust a work surface with cornmeal or flour. Place the pizza dough on the surface and gently stretch it into a round or rectangular shape, about 12-14 inches in diameter.

Prepare the Apple Topping:
- In a bowl, toss the thinly sliced apples with lemon juice to prevent browning.
- In a small bowl, mix together olive oil and ground cinnamon.

Assemble the Pizza:
- Transfer the stretched pizza dough to a pizza peel or parchment paper-lined baking sheet.
- Brush the olive oil and cinnamon mixture evenly over the dough.
- Arrange the thinly sliced apples evenly over the dough.
- Sprinkle shredded sharp cheddar cheese evenly over the apples.
- Drizzle honey over the pizza.

- Sprinkle chopped fresh thyme leaves over the top.
- Season lightly with salt and pepper.

Bake the Pizza:
- If using a pizza stone, carefully transfer the pizza from the peel to the preheated stone in the oven. If using a baking sheet, simply place the baking sheet in the oven.
- Bake the pizza for 10-12 minutes, or until the crust is golden brown and the cheese is melted and bubbly.

Finish and Serve:
- Remove the pizza from the oven and let it cool slightly.
- Slice the pizza and serve hot.

Notes:

- Feel free to customize your apple and cheddar pizza with additional toppings such as caramelized onions or crispy bacon.
- You can use store-bought or homemade pizza dough for this recipe.

Enjoy your delicious homemade apple and cheddar pizza!

Mushroom and Truffle Oil Pizza

Ingredients:

For the Pizza Dough:

- 1 pound (about 4 cups) pizza dough, store-bought or homemade
- Cornmeal or flour for dusting

For the Pizza Toppings:

- 1 tablespoon olive oil
- 1 pound mushrooms (such as cremini or button), thinly sliced
- 2 cloves garlic, minced
- Salt and pepper to taste
- 1 1/2 cups shredded mozzarella cheese
- 1/4 cup grated Parmesan cheese
- Truffle oil, for drizzling
- Fresh parsley, chopped, for garnish

Instructions:

Preheat the Oven:
- Preheat your oven to the highest temperature it can go, typically around 475-500°F (245-260°C). If you have a pizza stone, place it in the oven to preheat as well.

Prepare the Pizza Dough:
- Dust a work surface with cornmeal or flour. Place the pizza dough on the surface and gently stretch it into a round or rectangular shape, about 12-14 inches in diameter.

Prepare the Mushroom Topping:
- In a skillet, heat olive oil over medium heat. Add minced garlic and sauté for about 1 minute until fragrant.
- Add the thinly sliced mushrooms to the skillet. Season with salt and pepper to taste. Cook, stirring occasionally, until the mushrooms are golden brown and tender, about 5-6 minutes. Remove from heat and set aside.

Assemble the Pizza:
- Transfer the stretched pizza dough to a pizza peel or parchment paper-lined baking sheet.

- Spread shredded mozzarella cheese evenly over the dough, leaving a small border around the edges.
- Scatter the cooked mushrooms evenly over the cheese.
- Sprinkle grated Parmesan cheese over the top of the pizza.
- Drizzle truffle oil evenly over the pizza, to taste.

Bake the Pizza:
- If using a pizza stone, carefully transfer the pizza from the peel to the preheated stone in the oven. If using a baking sheet, simply place the baking sheet in the oven.
- Bake the pizza for 10-12 minutes, or until the crust is golden brown and the cheese is melted and bubbly.

Finish and Serve:
- Remove the pizza from the oven and let it cool slightly.
- Garnish with chopped fresh parsley.
- Slice the pizza and serve hot.

Notes:

- Truffle oil is potent, so use it sparingly to avoid overpowering the flavors of the pizza.
- Feel free to add additional toppings such as caramelized onions or roasted garlic to enhance the flavor of the pizza.
- You can use store-bought or homemade pizza dough for this recipe.

Enjoy your delicious homemade mushroom and truffle oil pizza!

Pear and Gorgonzola Pizza

Ingredients:

For the Pizza Dough:

- 1 pound (about 4 cups) pizza dough, store-bought or homemade
- Cornmeal or flour for dusting

For the Pizza Toppings:

- 2 ripe pears, thinly sliced
- 1 tablespoon lemon juice (to prevent browning)
- 1 tablespoon honey
- 1 cup crumbled Gorgonzola cheese
- 1 cup shredded mozzarella cheese
- 1/4 cup chopped walnuts or pecans
- Fresh thyme leaves, for garnish
- Red pepper flakes (optional)
- Salt and pepper to taste

Instructions:

Preheat the Oven:
- Preheat your oven to the highest temperature it can go, typically around 475-500°F (245-260°C). If you have a pizza stone, place it in the oven to preheat as well.

Prepare the Pizza Dough:
- Dust a work surface with cornmeal or flour. Place the pizza dough on the surface and gently stretch it into a round or rectangular shape, about 12-14 inches in diameter.

Prepare the Pear Toppings:
- In a bowl, toss the thinly sliced pears with lemon juice to prevent browning. Drain any excess lemon juice.

Assemble the Pizza:
- Transfer the stretched pizza dough to a pizza peel or parchment paper-lined baking sheet.
- Spread shredded mozzarella cheese evenly over the dough, leaving a small border around the edges.
- Arrange the thinly sliced pears evenly over the cheese.
- Sprinkle crumbled Gorgonzola cheese evenly over the pears.

- Drizzle honey over the pizza.
- Sprinkle chopped walnuts or pecans over the top.
- Season lightly with salt and pepper.
- Optionally, sprinkle red pepper flakes over the pizza for extra heat.

Bake the Pizza:
- If using a pizza stone, carefully transfer the pizza from the peel to the preheated stone in the oven. If using a baking sheet, simply place the baking sheet in the oven.
- Bake the pizza for 10-12 minutes, or until the crust is golden brown and the cheese is melted and bubbly.

Finish and Serve:
- Remove the pizza from the oven and let it cool slightly.
- Garnish with fresh thyme leaves.
- Slice the pizza and serve hot.

Notes:

- Feel free to customize your pear and Gorgonzola pizza with additional toppings such as caramelized onions or arugula.
- You can use store-bought or homemade pizza dough for this recipe.

Enjoy your delicious homemade pear and Gorgonzola pizza!

Swedish Meatball Pizza

Ingredients:

For the Pizza Dough:

- 1 pound (about 4 cups) pizza dough, store-bought or homemade
- Cornmeal or flour for dusting

For the Swedish Meatballs:

- 1 pound ground beef
- 1/2 cup breadcrumbs
- 1/4 cup milk
- 1 egg
- 1/4 cup grated Parmesan cheese
- 1/2 teaspoon salt
- 1/4 teaspoon black pepper
-
- 1/4 teaspoon ground nutmeg
- 1/4 teaspoon ground allspice
- 1/4 teaspoon ground ginger
- 1/4 cup chopped fresh parsley
- 1 tablespoon olive oil

For the Pizza Toppings:

- 1 cup marinara sauce
- 1 1/2 cups shredded mozzarella cheese
- 1/4 cup grated Parmesan cheese
- Fresh parsley, chopped, for garnish

Instructions:

Preheat the Oven:
- Preheat your oven to the highest temperature it can go, typically around 475-500°F (245-260°C). If you have a pizza stone, place it in the oven to preheat as well.

Prepare the Pizza Dough:
- Dust a work surface with cornmeal or flour. Place the pizza dough on the surface and gently stretch it into a round or rectangular shape, about 12-14 inches in diameter.

Prepare the Swedish Meatballs:
- In a large bowl, combine ground beef, breadcrumbs, milk, egg, grated Parmesan cheese, salt, pepper, nutmeg, allspice, ginger, and chopped parsley. Mix until well combined.
- Shape the mixture into small meatballs, about 1 inch in diameter.
- In a skillet, heat olive oil over medium heat. Add the meatballs and cook until browned on all sides and cooked through, about 8-10 minutes. Remove from heat and set aside.

Assemble the Pizza:
- Spread marinara sauce evenly over the stretched pizza dough, leaving a small border around the edges.
- Arrange the cooked Swedish meatballs evenly over the sauce.
- Sprinkle shredded mozzarella cheese evenly over the meatballs.
- Sprinkle grated Parmesan cheese over the top of the pizza.

Bake the Pizza:
- If using a pizza stone, carefully transfer the pizza from the peel to the preheated stone in the oven. If using a baking sheet, simply place the baking sheet in the oven.
- Bake the pizza for 10-12 minutes, or until the crust is golden brown and the cheese is melted and bubbly.

Finish and Serve:
- Remove the pizza from the oven and let it cool slightly.
- Garnish with chopped fresh parsley.
- Slice the pizza and serve hot.

Notes:

- Feel free to customize your Swedish meatball pizza with additional toppings such as caramelized onions or sliced mushrooms.
- You can use store-bought or homemade pizza dough for this recipe.

Enjoy your delicious homemade Swedish meatball pizza!

Chicken Caesar Pizza

Ingredients:

For the Pizza Dough:

- 1 pound (about 4 cups) pizza dough, store-bought or homemade
- Cornmeal or flour for dusting

For the Pizza Toppings:

- 1 boneless, skinless chicken breast
- Salt and pepper to taste
- Olive oil for cooking
- 1/2 cup Caesar dressing
- 1 cup shredded mozzarella cheese
- 1/4 cup grated Parmesan cheese
- 1 cup chopped romaine lettuce
- 1/4 cup sliced cherry tomatoes
- 1/4 cup croutons
- Freshly ground black pepper
- Fresh parsley, chopped, for garnish

Instructions:

Preheat the Oven:
- Preheat your oven to the highest temperature it can go, typically around 475-500°F (245-260°C). If you have a pizza stone, place it in the oven to preheat as well.

Prepare the Chicken:
- Season the chicken breast with salt and pepper on both sides.
- In a skillet, heat olive oil over medium-high heat. Add the chicken breast and cook until golden brown and cooked through, about 5-6 minutes per side. Remove from heat and let it cool slightly, then thinly slice.

Prepare the Pizza Dough:
- Dust a work surface with cornmeal or flour. Place the pizza dough on the surface and gently stretch it into a round or rectangular shape, about 12-14 inches in diameter.

Assemble the Pizza:
- Transfer the stretched pizza dough to a pizza peel or parchment paper-lined baking sheet.

- Spread Caesar dressing evenly over the dough, leaving a small border around the edges.
- Sprinkle shredded mozzarella cheese evenly over the dressing.
- Arrange the sliced chicken breast over the cheese.
- Sprinkle grated Parmesan cheese over the top of the pizza.
- Bake the pizza in the preheated oven for 10-12 minutes, or until the crust is golden brown and the cheese is melted and bubbly.

Finish and Serve:
- Remove the pizza from the oven and let it cool slightly.
- Top the pizza with chopped romaine lettuce, sliced cherry tomatoes, and croutons.
- Sprinkle freshly ground black pepper over the top.
- Garnish with chopped fresh parsley.
- Slice the pizza and serve hot.

Notes:

- You can customize your Chicken Caesar pizza by adding other toppings like bacon or red onions.
- You can use store-bought or homemade Caesar dressing for this recipe.

Enjoy your delicious homemade Chicken Caesar pizza!

Kimchi Pizza

Ingredients:

For the Pizza Dough:

- 1 pound (about 4 cups) pizza dough, store-bought or homemade
- Cornmeal or flour for dusting

For the Pizza Toppings:

- 1 cup kimchi, drained and chopped
- 1 tablespoon sesame oil
- 1 tablespoon soy sauce
- 1 cup shredded mozzarella cheese
- 1/4 cup grated Parmesan cheese
- 2 green onions, thinly sliced
- 1 tablespoon sesame seeds
- Red pepper flakes (optional)

Instructions:

Preheat the Oven:
- Preheat your oven to the highest temperature it can go, typically around 475-500°F (245-260°C). If you have a pizza stone, place it in the oven to preheat as well.

Prepare the Pizza Dough:
- Dust a work surface with cornmeal or flour. Place the pizza dough on the surface and gently stretch it into a round or rectangular shape, about 12-14 inches in diameter.

Prepare the Kimchi Topping:
- In a small bowl, mix together the chopped kimchi, sesame oil, and soy sauce until well combined.

Assemble the Pizza:
- Transfer the stretched pizza dough to a pizza peel or parchment paper-lined baking sheet.
- Spread the kimchi mixture evenly over the dough, leaving a small border around the edges.
- Sprinkle shredded mozzarella cheese evenly over the kimchi.
- Sprinkle grated Parmesan cheese over the top of the pizza.
- Scatter thinly sliced green onions over the pizza.

- Sprinkle sesame seeds evenly over the pizza.
- Optionally, sprinkle red pepper flakes over the pizza for extra heat.

Bake the Pizza:
- If using a pizza stone, carefully transfer the pizza from the peel to the preheated stone in the oven. If using a baking sheet, simply place the baking sheet in the oven.
- Bake the pizza for 10-12 minutes, or until the crust is golden brown and the cheese is melted and bubbly.

Finish and Serve:
- Remove the pizza from the oven and let it cool slightly.
- Slice the pizza and serve hot.

Notes:

- Feel free to customize your kimchi pizza with additional toppings such as cooked chicken, pork, or tofu.
- You can find kimchi in the refrigerated section of most grocery stores or at Asian markets.
- You can use store-bought or homemade pizza dough for this recipe.

Enjoy your delicious homemade kimchi pizza!

Breakfast Pizza with Sausage and Egg

Ingredients:

For the Pizza Dough:

- 1 pound (about 4 cups) pizza dough, store-bought or homemade
- Cornmeal or flour for dusting

For the Pizza Toppings:

- 1/2 pound breakfast sausage, cooked and crumbled
- 4 large eggs
- 1 cup shredded mozzarella cheese
- 1/4 cup grated Parmesan cheese
- Salt and pepper to taste
- 2 green onions, thinly sliced (optional)
- Red pepper flakes (optional)

Instructions:

Preheat the Oven:
- Preheat your oven to the highest temperature it can go, typically around 475-500°F (245-260°C). If you have a pizza stone, place it in the oven to preheat as well.

Prepare the Pizza Dough:
- Dust a work surface with cornmeal or flour. Place the pizza dough on the surface and gently stretch it into a round or rectangular shape, about 12-14 inches in diameter.

Assemble the Pizza:
- Transfer the stretched pizza dough to a pizza peel or parchment paper-lined baking sheet.
- Spread the cooked and crumbled breakfast sausage evenly over the dough.
- Sprinkle shredded mozzarella cheese evenly over the sausage.
- Create four small wells in the cheese and sausage mixture for the eggs.
- Crack one egg into each well.
- Sprinkle grated Parmesan cheese over the top of the pizza.
- Season the eggs with salt and pepper to taste.
- Optionally, sprinkle thinly sliced green onions and red pepper flakes over the pizza for extra flavor.

Bake the Pizza:
- If using a pizza stone, carefully transfer the pizza from the peel to the preheated stone in the oven. If using a baking sheet, simply place the baking sheet in the oven.
- Bake the pizza for 10-12 minutes, or until the crust is golden brown, the cheese is melted, and the eggs are cooked to your desired level of doneness.

Finish and Serve:
- Remove the pizza from the oven and let it cool slightly.
- Slice the pizza and serve hot.

Notes:

- Feel free to customize your breakfast pizza with additional toppings such as cooked bacon, ham, or vegetables.
- Make sure to spread the toppings evenly on the pizza dough to ensure even cooking.
- You can use store-bought or homemade pizza dough for this recipe.

Enjoy your delicious homemade breakfast pizza with sausage and egg!

Smoked Trout Pizza

Ingredients:

For the Pizza Dough:

- 1 pound (about 4 cups) pizza dough, store-bought or homemade
- Cornmeal or flour for dusting

For the Pizza Toppings:

- 8 ounces smoked trout, flaked into small pieces
- 1/2 cup crème fraîche or sour cream
- 1 tablespoon fresh dill, chopped
- 1 tablespoon capers, drained
- 1 small red onion, thinly sliced
- 1 tablespoon olive oil
- Salt and pepper to taste
- Lemon wedges, for serving
- Fresh arugula, for garnish (optional)

Instructions:

Preheat the Oven:
- Preheat your oven to the highest temperature it can go, typically around 475-500°F (245-260°C). If you have a pizza stone, place it in the oven to preheat as well.

Prepare the Pizza Dough:
- Dust a work surface with cornmeal or flour. Place the pizza dough on the surface and gently stretch it into a round or rectangular shape, about 12-14 inches in diameter.

Assemble the Pizza:
- Transfer the stretched pizza dough to a pizza peel or parchment paper-lined baking sheet.
- In a small bowl, mix together the crème fraîche (or sour cream) and chopped fresh dill. Spread this mixture evenly over the pizza dough, leaving a small border around the edges.
- Scatter the flaked smoked trout evenly over the crème fraîche mixture.
- Sprinkle drained capers and thinly sliced red onion over the top of the pizza.
- Drizzle olive oil over the pizza.

- Season lightly with salt and pepper.

Bake the Pizza:
- If using a pizza stone, carefully transfer the pizza from the peel to the preheated stone in the oven. If using a baking sheet, simply place the baking sheet in the oven.
- Bake the pizza for 10-12 minutes, or until the crust is golden brown and the toppings are heated through.

Finish and Serve:
- Remove the pizza from the oven and let it cool slightly.
- Garnish with fresh arugula, if desired.
- Serve hot with lemon wedges on the side.

Notes:

- Smoked trout can be found in the seafood section of most grocery stores or at specialty markets.
- Feel free to customize your smoked trout pizza with additional toppings such as sliced tomatoes or shredded cheese.
- You can use store-bought or homemade pizza dough for this recipe.

Enjoy your delicious homemade smoked trout pizza!

Grilled Vegetable and Hummus Pizza

Ingredients:

For the Pizza Dough:

- 1 pound (about 4 cups) pizza dough, store-bought or homemade
- Cornmeal or flour for dusting

For the Pizza Toppings:

- 1 cup hummus (store-bought or homemade)
- 1 medium zucchini, sliced
- 1 medium yellow squash, sliced
- 1 bell pepper, sliced (any color)
- 1 red onion, sliced
- 1 cup cherry tomatoes, halved
- 2 tablespoons olive oil
- Salt and pepper to taste
- 1/2 cup crumbled feta cheese (optional)
- Fresh basil leaves, chopped, for garnish

Instructions:

Preheat the Grill:
- Preheat your grill to medium-high heat.

Prepare the Pizza Dough:
- Dust a work surface with cornmeal or flour. Place the pizza dough on the surface and gently stretch it into a round or rectangular shape, about 12-14 inches in diameter.

Grill the Vegetables:
- In a large bowl, toss the sliced zucchini, yellow squash, bell pepper, red onion, and cherry tomatoes with olive oil. Season with salt and pepper to taste.
- Grill the vegetables for 3-4 minutes per side, or until they are tender and have grill marks. Remove from the grill and set aside.

Assemble the Pizza:
- Transfer the stretched pizza dough to a pizza peel or parchment paper-lined baking sheet.
- Spread the hummus evenly over the dough, leaving a small border around the edges.

- Arrange the grilled vegetables evenly over the hummus.
- If using, sprinkle crumbled feta cheese evenly over the vegetables.

Grill the Pizza:
- If using a pizza stone, carefully transfer the pizza from the peel to the preheated stone on the grill. If using a baking sheet, place the baking sheet directly on the grill.
- Close the grill lid and cook the pizza for 8-10 minutes, or until the crust is golden brown and the toppings are heated through.

Finish and Serve:
- Remove the pizza from the grill and let it cool slightly.
- Garnish with chopped fresh basil leaves.
- Slice the pizza and serve hot.

Notes:

- Feel free to customize your grilled vegetable and hummus pizza with additional toppings such as olives, artichoke hearts, or pine nuts.
- You can use store-bought or homemade pizza dough for this recipe.
- If you don't have a grill, you can also bake the pizza in a preheated oven at 475°F (245°C) for 10-12 minutes, or until the crust is golden brown and the toppings are heated through.

Enjoy your delicious homemade grilled vegetable and hummus pizza!

Pastrami and Swiss Pizza

Ingredients:

For the Pizza Dough:

- 1 pound (about 4 cups) pizza dough, store-bought or homemade
- Cornmeal or flour for dusting

For the Pizza Toppings:

- 1/2 pound thinly sliced pastrami
- 1 cup shredded Swiss cheese
- 1/4 cup Dijon mustard
- 1/4 cup thinly sliced red onion
- 2 tablespoons chopped fresh dill (optional)
- Olive oil for drizzling
- Salt and pepper to taste

Instructions:

Preheat the Oven:
- Preheat your oven to the highest temperature it can go, typically around 475-500°F (245-260°C). If you have a pizza stone, place it in the oven to preheat as well.

Prepare the Pizza Dough:
- Dust a work surface with cornmeal or flour. Place the pizza dough on the surface and gently stretch it into a round or rectangular shape, about 12-14 inches in diameter.

Assemble the Pizza:
- Transfer the stretched pizza dough to a pizza peel or parchment paper-lined baking sheet.
- Spread Dijon mustard evenly over the dough, leaving a small border around the edges.
- Arrange the thinly sliced pastrami evenly over the mustard.
- Sprinkle shredded Swiss cheese evenly over the pastrami.
- Scatter thinly sliced red onion over the top of the pizza.
- Optionally, sprinkle chopped fresh dill over the pizza for extra flavor.
- Drizzle olive oil over the pizza.
- Season lightly with salt and pepper.

Bake the Pizza:
- If using a pizza stone, carefully transfer the pizza from the peel to the preheated stone in the oven. If using a baking sheet, simply place the baking sheet in the oven.
- Bake the pizza for 10-12 minutes, or until the crust is golden brown and the cheese is melted and bubbly.

Finish and Serve:
- Remove the pizza from the oven and let it cool slightly.
- Slice the pizza and serve hot.

Notes:

- Feel free to customize your pastrami and Swiss pizza with additional toppings such as sliced pickles or sauerkraut.
- You can use store-bought or homemade pizza dough for this recipe.

Enjoy your delicious homemade pastrami and Swiss pizza!

Steak and Blue Cheese Pizza

Ingredients:

For the Pizza Dough:

- 1 pound (about 4 cups) pizza dough, store-bought or homemade
- Cornmeal or flour for dusting

For the Pizza Toppings:

- 8 ounces steak (such as ribeye or sirloin), thinly sliced
- Salt and pepper to taste
- 1 tablespoon olive oil
- 1/2 cup crumbled blue cheese
- 1 cup shredded mozzarella cheese
- 1/4 cup grated Parmesan cheese
- 1/4 cup caramelized onions (optional)
- Fresh arugula, for garnish (optional)
- Balsamic glaze, for drizzling (optional)

Instructions:

Preheat the Oven:
- Preheat your oven to the highest temperature it can go, typically around 475-500°F (245-260°C). If you have a pizza stone, place it in the oven to preheat as well.

Prepare the Pizza Dough:
- Dust a work surface with cornmeal or flour. Place the pizza dough on the surface and gently stretch it into a round or rectangular shape, about 12-14 inches in diameter.

Cook the Steak:
- Season the thinly sliced steak with salt and pepper to taste.
- In a skillet, heat olive oil over medium-high heat. Add the steak slices and cook for 2-3 minutes per side, or until cooked to your desired level of doneness. Remove from heat and set aside.

Assemble the Pizza:
- Transfer the stretched pizza dough to a pizza peel or parchment paper-lined baking sheet.

- Spread shredded mozzarella cheese evenly over the dough, leaving a small border around the edges.
- Arrange the cooked steak slices evenly over the cheese.
- Sprinkle crumbled blue cheese evenly over the steak.
- If using, scatter caramelized onions over the top of the pizza.
- Sprinkle grated Parmesan cheese over the pizza.

Bake the Pizza:

- If using a pizza stone, carefully transfer the pizza from the peel to the preheated stone in the oven. If using a baking sheet, simply place the baking sheet in the oven.
- Bake the pizza for 10-12 minutes, or until the crust is golden brown and the cheese is melted and bubbly.

Finish and Serve:

- Remove the pizza from the oven and let it cool slightly.
- Garnish with fresh arugula, if desired.
- Drizzle balsamic glaze over the top of the pizza, if desired.
- Slice the pizza and serve hot.

Notes:

- Feel free to customize your steak and blue cheese pizza with additional toppings such as roasted mushrooms or caramelized onions.
- You can use store-bought or homemade pizza dough for this recipe.

Enjoy your delicious homemade steak and blue cheese pizza!

Ratatouille Pizza

Ingredients:

For the Pizza Dough:

- 1 pound (about 4 cups) pizza dough, store-bought or homemade
- Cornmeal or flour for dusting

For the Ratatouille Topping:

- 1 small eggplant, thinly sliced
- 1 small zucchini, thinly sliced
- 1 small yellow squash, thinly sliced
- 1 bell pepper (any color), thinly sliced
- 1 small red onion, thinly sliced
- 2 cloves garlic, minced
- 2 tablespoons olive oil
- 1 cup marinara sauce
- 1 cup shredded mozzarella cheese
- Salt and pepper to taste
- Fresh basil leaves, chopped, for garnish

Instructions:

Preheat the Oven:
- Preheat your oven to the highest temperature it can go, typically around 475-500°F (245-260°C). If you have a pizza stone, place it in the oven to preheat as well.

Prepare the Ratatouille Topping:
- In a large skillet, heat olive oil over medium heat. Add minced garlic and sauté for 1 minute, until fragrant.
- Add the thinly sliced eggplant, zucchini, yellow squash, bell pepper, and red onion to the skillet. Season with salt and pepper to taste. Cook, stirring occasionally, for about 5-7 minutes, or until the vegetables are tender. Remove from heat and set aside.

Prepare the Pizza Dough:
- Dust a work surface with cornmeal or flour. Place the pizza dough on the surface and gently stretch it into a round or rectangular shape, about 12-14 inches in diameter.

Assemble the Pizza:

- Transfer the stretched pizza dough to a pizza peel or parchment paper-lined baking sheet.
- Spread marinara sauce evenly over the dough, leaving a small border around the edges.
- Arrange the cooked ratatouille vegetables evenly over the sauce.
- Sprinkle shredded mozzarella cheese evenly over the vegetables.

Bake the Pizza:
- If using a pizza stone, carefully transfer the pizza from the peel to the preheated stone in the oven. If using a baking sheet, simply place the baking sheet in the oven.
- Bake the pizza for 10-12 minutes, or until the crust is golden brown and the cheese is melted and bubbly.

Finish and Serve:
- Remove the pizza from the oven and let it cool slightly.
- Garnish with chopped fresh basil leaves.
- Slice the pizza and serve hot.

Notes:

- Ratatouille pizza is a great way to use up seasonal vegetables. Feel free to customize the toppings based on what you have on hand.
- You can use store-bought or homemade pizza dough for this recipe.

Enjoy your delicious homemade ratatouille pizza!

Curry Chicken Pizza

Ingredients:

For the Pizza Dough:

- 1 pound (about 4 cups) pizza dough, store-bought or homemade
- Cornmeal or flour for dusting

For the Curry Chicken Topping:

- 1 pound boneless, skinless chicken breasts, cut into small cubes
- 2 tablespoons curry powder
- 1 teaspoon ground cumin
- 1 teaspoon ground coriander
- 1/2 teaspoon turmeric
- 1/2 teaspoon paprika
- 1/4 teaspoon cayenne pepper (optional, for extra heat)
- Salt and pepper to taste
- 2 tablespoons olive oil
- 1 small onion, finely chopped
- 2 cloves garlic, minced
- 1/2 cup tomato sauce or crushed tomatoes
- 1/4 cup coconut milk
- 1 cup shredded mozzarella cheese
- Fresh cilantro, chopped, for garnish

Instructions:

Preheat the Oven:
- Preheat your oven to the highest temperature it can go, typically around 475-500°F (245-260°C). If you have a pizza stone, place it in the oven to preheat as well.

Prepare the Curry Chicken:
- In a mixing bowl, combine the chicken cubes with curry powder, ground cumin, ground coriander, turmeric, paprika, cayenne pepper (if using), salt, and pepper. Toss until the chicken is evenly coated with the spices.
- In a skillet, heat olive oil over medium-high heat. Add the chopped onion and minced garlic, and sauté until softened and fragrant, about 2-3 minutes.

- Add the seasoned chicken cubes to the skillet and cook until browned and cooked through, about 6-8 minutes.
- Stir in the tomato sauce or crushed tomatoes and coconut milk. Simmer for another 2-3 minutes until the sauce thickens slightly. Remove from heat and set aside.

Prepare the Pizza Dough:
- Dust a work surface with cornmeal or flour. Place the pizza dough on the surface and gently stretch it into a round or rectangular shape, about 12-14 inches in diameter.

Assemble the Pizza:
- Transfer the stretched pizza dough to a pizza peel or parchment paper-lined baking sheet.
- Spread the curry chicken mixture evenly over the dough, leaving a small border around the edges.
- Sprinkle shredded mozzarella cheese evenly over the chicken.

Bake the Pizza:
- If using a pizza stone, carefully transfer the pizza from the peel to the preheated stone in the oven. If using a baking sheet, simply place the baking sheet in the oven.
- Bake the pizza for 10-12 minutes, or until the crust is golden brown and the cheese is melted and bubbly.

Finish and Serve:
- Remove the pizza from the oven and let it cool slightly.
- Garnish with chopped fresh cilantro.
- Slice the pizza and serve hot.

Notes:

- Feel free to customize your curry chicken pizza with additional toppings such as sliced bell peppers, red onions, or pineapple.
- You can use store-bought or homemade pizza dough for this recipe.

Enjoy your delicious homemade curry chicken pizza!

Avocado and Bacon Pizza

Ingredients:

For the Pizza Dough:

- 1 pound (about 4 cups) pizza dough, store-bought or homemade
- Cornmeal or flour for dusting

For the Pizza Toppings:

- 1 ripe avocado, sliced
- 6 slices of bacon, cooked until crispy and crumbled
- 1 cup shredded mozzarella cheese
- 1/4 cup grated Parmesan cheese
- 2 cloves garlic, minced
- 1 tablespoon olive oil
- Red pepper flakes (optional)
- Salt and pepper to taste
- Fresh cilantro or basil leaves, chopped, for garnish

Instructions:

Preheat the Oven:
- Preheat your oven to the highest temperature it can go, typically around 475-500°F (245-260°C). If you have a pizza stone, place it in the oven to preheat as well.

Prepare the Pizza Dough:
- Dust a work surface with cornmeal or flour. Place the pizza dough on the surface and gently stretch it into a round or rectangular shape, about 12-14 inches in diameter.

Assemble the Pizza:
- Transfer the stretched pizza dough to a pizza peel or parchment paper-lined baking sheet.
- In a small bowl, mix together minced garlic and olive oil. Brush this mixture evenly over the surface of the dough.
- Sprinkle shredded mozzarella cheese evenly over the dough, leaving a small border around the edges.
- Arrange the sliced avocado over the cheese.
- Sprinkle the crumbled bacon over the avocado.

- Sprinkle grated Parmesan cheese over the top of the pizza.
- Optionally, sprinkle red pepper flakes over the pizza for extra heat.
- Season lightly with salt and pepper to taste.

Bake the Pizza:
- If using a pizza stone, carefully transfer the pizza from the peel to the preheated stone in the oven. If using a baking sheet, simply place the baking sheet in the oven.
- Bake the pizza for 10-12 minutes, or until the crust is golden brown and the cheese is melted and bubbly.

Finish and Serve:
- Remove the pizza from the oven and let it cool slightly.
- Garnish with chopped fresh cilantro or basil leaves.
- Slice the pizza and serve hot.

Notes:

- Feel free to customize your avocado and bacon pizza with additional toppings such as cherry tomatoes, red onions, or arugula.
- You can use store-bought or homemade pizza dough for this recipe.

Enjoy your delicious homemade avocado and bacon pizza!

Brussels Sprouts and Pancetta Pizza

Ingredients:

For the Pizza Dough:

- 1 pound (about 4 cups) pizza dough, store-bought or homemade
- Cornmeal or flour for dusting

For the Pizza Toppings:

- 6 ounces pancetta, diced
- 1 pound Brussels sprouts, trimmed and thinly sliced
- 2 tablespoons olive oil
- Salt and pepper to taste
- 1 cup shredded mozzarella cheese
- 1/4 cup grated Parmesan cheese
- 2 cloves garlic, minced
- Red pepper flakes (optional)
- Balsamic glaze, for drizzling (optional)
- Fresh parsley, chopped, for garnish

Instructions:

Preheat the Oven:
- Preheat your oven to the highest temperature it can go, typically around 475-500°F (245-260°C). If you have a pizza stone, place it in the oven to preheat as well.

Prepare the Pizza Dough:
- Dust a work surface with cornmeal or flour. Place the pizza dough on the surface and gently stretch it into a round or rectangular shape, about 12-14 inches in diameter.

Prepare the Brussels Sprouts and Pancetta:
- In a large skillet, cook the diced pancetta over medium heat until crispy. Remove the pancetta from the skillet and set it aside.
- In the same skillet, add the thinly sliced Brussels sprouts and olive oil. Season with salt and pepper to taste. Cook, stirring occasionally, until the Brussels sprouts are tender and slightly caramelized, about 8-10 minutes. Remove from heat and set aside.

Assemble the Pizza:

- Transfer the stretched pizza dough to a pizza peel or parchment paper-lined baking sheet.
- In a small bowl, mix together minced garlic and a drizzle of olive oil. Brush this mixture evenly over the surface of the dough.
- Sprinkle shredded mozzarella cheese evenly over the dough, leaving a small border around the edges.
- Spread the cooked Brussels sprouts evenly over the cheese.
- Sprinkle the crispy pancetta over the Brussels sprouts.
- Sprinkle grated Parmesan cheese over the top of the pizza.
- Optionally, sprinkle red pepper flakes over the pizza for extra heat.

Bake the Pizza:

- If using a pizza stone, carefully transfer the pizza from the peel to the preheated stone in the oven. If using a baking sheet, simply place the baking sheet in the oven.
- Bake the pizza for 10-12 minutes, or until the crust is golden brown and the cheese is melted and bubbly.

Finish and Serve:

- Remove the pizza from the oven and let it cool slightly.
- Drizzle balsamic glaze over the top of the pizza, if desired.
- Garnish with chopped fresh parsley.
- Slice the pizza and serve hot.

Notes:

- You can use store-bought or homemade pizza dough for this recipe.
- Feel free to customize your Brussels sprouts and pancetta pizza with additional toppings such as caramelized onions or goat cheese.

Enjoy your delicious homemade Brussels sprouts and pancetta pizza!

Beet and Goat Cheese Pizza

Ingredients:

For the Pizza Dough:

- 1 pound (about 4 cups) pizza dough, store-bought or homemade
- Cornmeal or flour for dusting

For the Pizza Toppings:

- 2 medium-sized beets, cooked, peeled, and thinly sliced
- 4 ounces goat cheese, crumbled
- 1/4 cup chopped walnuts
- 1 tablespoon honey
- 2 tablespoons olive oil
- Salt and pepper to taste
- Fresh thyme leaves for garnish (optional)
- Arugula or baby spinach for serving (optional)

Instructions:

Preheat the Oven:
- Preheat your oven to the highest temperature it can go, typically around 475-500°F (245-260°C). If you have a pizza stone, place it in the oven to preheat as well.

Prepare the Pizza Dough:
- Dust a work surface with cornmeal or flour. Place the pizza dough on the surface and gently stretch it into a round or rectangular shape, about 12-14 inches in diameter.

Assemble the Pizza:
- Transfer the stretched pizza dough to a pizza peel or parchment paper-lined baking sheet.
- Brush olive oil evenly over the surface of the dough.
- Arrange the thinly sliced beets evenly over the dough.
- Sprinkle crumbled goat cheese evenly over the beets.
- Sprinkle chopped walnuts evenly over the pizza.
- Drizzle honey evenly over the top of the pizza.
- Season lightly with salt and pepper to taste.

Bake the Pizza:

- If using a pizza stone, carefully transfer the pizza from the peel to the preheated stone in the oven. If using a baking sheet, simply place the baking sheet in the oven.
- Bake the pizza for 10-12 minutes, or until the crust is golden brown and the cheese is melted and bubbly.

Finish and Serve:
- Remove the pizza from the oven and let it cool slightly.
- Garnish with fresh thyme leaves, if desired.
- Serve hot, optionally topped with arugula or baby spinach for some extra freshness.

Notes:

- You can cook the beets ahead of time by roasting or boiling them until tender, then allowing them to cool before slicing.
- Feel free to add a balsamic glaze drizzle over the pizza for an extra layer of flavor.
- You can use store-bought or homemade pizza dough for this recipe.

Enjoy your delicious homemade beet and goat cheese pizza!

Lingonberry and Brie Pizza

Ingredients:

For the Pizza Dough:

- 1 pound (about 4 cups) pizza dough, store-bought or homemade
- Cornmeal or flour for dusting

For the Pizza Toppings:

- 1/2 cup lingonberry preserves
- 6 ounces brie cheese, thinly sliced
- 1/4 cup chopped walnuts
- Fresh thyme leaves for garnish
- Honey for drizzling (optional)
- Arugula or baby spinach for serving (optional)

Instructions:

Preheat the Oven:
- Preheat your oven to the highest temperature it can go, typically around 475-500°F (245-260°C). If you have a pizza stone, place it in the oven to preheat as well.

Prepare the Pizza Dough:
- Dust a work surface with cornmeal or flour. Place the pizza dough on the surface and gently stretch it into a round or rectangular shape, about 12-14 inches in diameter.

Assemble the Pizza:
- Transfer the stretched pizza dough to a pizza peel or parchment paper-lined baking sheet.
- Spread lingonberry preserves evenly over the surface of the dough, leaving a small border around the edges.
- Arrange the thinly sliced brie cheese evenly over the lingonberry preserves.
- Sprinkle chopped walnuts evenly over the pizza.

Bake the Pizza:
- If using a pizza stone, carefully transfer the pizza from the peel to the preheated stone in the oven. If using a baking sheet, simply place the baking sheet in the oven.
- Bake the pizza for 10-12 minutes, or until the crust is golden brown and the cheese is melted and bubbly.

Finish and Serve:
- Remove the pizza from the oven and let it cool slightly.
- Garnish with fresh thyme leaves.
- Optionally, drizzle honey over the top of the pizza for an extra touch of sweetness.
- Serve hot, optionally topped with arugula or baby spinach for some extra freshness.

Notes:

- Lingonberry preserves can usually be found in the jam or international foods section of grocery stores. If you can't find lingonberry preserves, you can substitute with cranberry sauce or raspberry preserves.
- Feel free to add some thinly sliced red onions or prosciutto for additional flavor.
- You can use store-bought or homemade pizza dough for this recipe.

Enjoy your delicious homemade lingonberry and brie pizza!

www.ingramcontent.com/pod-product-compliance
Lightning Source LLC
LaVergne TN
LVHW061940070526
838199LV00060B/3895